Slovakia

Everything You Need
to Know

traditions, folklore, and the enduring spirit of community. Traditional Slovak cuisine, with its hearty and flavorful dishes, reflects the country's agricultural roots and the resourcefulness of its people.

Slovakia's natural beauty is a source of national pride, from the dense forests and pristine lakes of the Low Tatras to the enchanting caves of the Slovak Karst. The country is also home to an array of wildlife, including brown bears, lynx, and the iconic Tatra chamois.

As we journey through this book, we will delve deeper into the history, culture, cities, cuisine, language, and diverse landscapes of Slovakia. Each chapter will offer a glimpse into the multifaceted facets of this remarkable country, allowing you to explore its past, present, and the promising future that lies ahead. Slovakia beckons with open arms, inviting you to discover its hidden treasures and immerse yourself in its unique charm.

Geography and Landscapes

Slovakia's geography is a captivating mosaic of natural beauty that leaves an indelible mark on all who visit this Central European gem. Situated between 47° and 49° latitude north and 16° and 24° longitude east, Slovakia spans a relatively compact area of approximately 49,000 square kilometers, making it a relatively small European nation in terms of landmass. However, within this relatively modest space, it boasts a remarkable variety of landscapes and geographical features.

To the north, the imposing High Tatras reign as the tallest peaks in the Carpathian Mountain range, marking Slovakia's border with Poland. These rugged mountains offer not only breathtaking scenery but also a haven for outdoor enthusiasts, with pristine alpine lakes, challenging hiking trails, and opportunities for winter sports such as skiing and snowboarding. The High Tatras, with their towering summits like Gerlachovský štít, stand as a testament to Slovakia's natural grandeur.

As one journeys southward from the High Tatras, the terrain gradually transitions into the Low Tatras, a sprawling range characterized by rolling hills, dense forests, and an abundance of wildlife. This region is a playground for those seeking tranquility amid nature's splendor. The Low Tatras provide ample hiking, biking, and cross-country skiing opportunities, all set against the backdrop of unspoiled landscapes.

The Carpathian Mountains, which traverse much of Slovakia, are not only known for their scenic beauty but also their rich biodiversity. Slovakia's forests, which cover over 40% of its territory, shelter various species of flora and fauna, including the European brown bear, Eurasian lynx, and numerous bird species. The country's commitment to conservation is evident in its national parks and protected areas, which ensure the preservation of its natural heritage.

Slovakia's southern regions offer a contrast to the mountainous north, with rolling plains and fertile valleys. The Danube River flows through the capital city, Bratislava, before continuing its course along the southern border, providing a vital waterway for transportation and contributing to the country's agricultural productivity.

In addition to its mountains and lowlands, Slovakia boasts a network of enchanting caves, with the Domica Cave and the Dobsinska Ice Cave being notable examples. These subterranean wonders offer a unique perspective on the country's geological diversity.

In summary, Slovakia's geography is a treasure trove of natural wonders, from its towering peaks to its serene valleys, from its dense forests to its hidden caves. This varied landscape not only shapes the country's identity but also offers an array of recreational opportunities for both residents and visitors alike.

Historical Roots of Slovakia

The historical roots of Slovakia run deep, tracing back through the annals of time to the very origins of European civilization. This land, nestled in the heart of Central Europe, has witnessed the rise and fall of numerous empires and kingdoms, each leaving its indelible mark on the tapestry of Slovak history.

The earliest inhabitants of what is now Slovakia were the Celts, who settled in the region around the 4th century BC. Their presence is attested to by archaeological findings, including intricate jewelry and weaponry. Following the Celts, the Romans established a presence in the area, primarily for trade and military purposes. Roman artifacts and fortifications have been discovered, evidence of their influence on the land.

In the early centuries of the first millennium AD, the Slavic peoples began to migrate into the region, bringing with them their language and culture. This marked the beginning of a Slavic presence that would become integral to the identity of Slovakia. Over time, these Slavic tribes organized into larger political entities, setting the stage for the formation of the Great Moravian Empire in the 9th century. Great Moravia, with its capital in Nitra, played a pivotal role in the spread of Christianity in the region and left a lasting cultural legacy.

The 10th century saw Hungary's ascendancy, as it gradually incorporated the territories of present-day Slovakia into the Kingdom of Hungary. This period witnessed significant cultural and political exchange, as well as the gradual assimilation of Slovaks into the Hungarian kingdom. The Kingdom of Hungary held sway over Slovakia for nearly a thousand years, shaping its history, culture, and institutions.

Throughout the Middle Ages, Slovakia's cities flourished as centers of trade and culture. Bratislava, then known as Pressburg, became a bustling hub of commerce and a coronation site for Hungarian kings. Other towns, such as Kosice and Banska Bystrica, grew in prominence, bearing witness to the changing tides of history.

The 20th century brought profound changes to Slovakia's fate. After World War I, the dissolution of the Austro-Hungarian Empire gave birth to Czechoslovakia, a new nation that united Czechs and Slovaks. This union endured for several decades, marked by periods of cooperation and tension.

The latter half of the 20th century saw the establishment of a communist regime in Czechoslovakia, which lasted until the Velvet Revolution of 1989. This peaceful revolution, led by figures like Vaclav Havel and Alexander Dubcek, paved the way for the country's transition to democracy and the eventual dissolution of Czechoslovakia into the independent states of the Czech Republic and Slovakia in 1993.

Medieval Slovakia: Kingdom of Hungary

In the medieval era, Slovakia found itself intricately woven into the tapestry of the Kingdom of Hungary, a historical chapter that would leave a lasting imprint on the land and its people. This period, spanning several centuries, was marked by political dynamics, cultural exchanges, and territorial developments that would shape the course of Slovak history.

The Kingdom of Hungary, with its capital in Budapest, extended its dominion over the territories of present-day Slovakia in the early Middle Ages. It was during this time that the region became part of a larger European framework, as the Hungarian kings sought to expand their realm. This integration into Hungary brought about significant changes in governance, language, and culture, as the Hungarian nobility exerted their influence over the Slovak lands.

One of the defining features of this period was the introduction of feudalism, a socio-economic system characterized by a hierarchy of landownership and servitude. Large estates and castles dotted the Slovak landscape, with powerful nobles, both Hungarian and Slovak, presiding over their domains. This feudal structure shaped the lives of the common people, who often toiled as peasants on the land of their lords.

The medieval period also saw the spread of Christianity in Slovakia. The influence of the Roman Catholic Church grew, as monasteries and churches were established across the land. The arrival of Christianity brought not only religious transformation but also cultural and educational advancements, with monasteries serving as centers of learning and preservation of written knowledge.

Slovakia's cities, such as Bratislava and Kosice, flourished as key trade and cultural centers within the Hungarian kingdom. The bustling markets and merchant guilds played a pivotal role in connecting Slovakia with wider European trade routes. These urban centers also bore witness to the interplay of diverse cultures, as merchants and travelers from across Europe converged in the heart of Slovakia.

The medieval era was not without its challenges. Slovakia, situated at the crossroads of various empires and kingdoms, often found itself caught in the midst of power struggles and conflicts. Invasions by Mongols, Ottoman Turks, and other external forces left their mark on the land, leading to periods of turmoil and upheaval.

As time progressed, the Hungarian crown sought to strengthen its control over the Slovak territories, leading to a process of assimilation. The Slovak identity persisted, though, as the people maintained their language, customs, and traditions.

The medieval period in Slovakia, under the rule of the Kingdom of Hungary, laid the foundation for the country's subsequent history. It left an enduring legacy of architectural marvels, religious heritage, and a cultural fusion that continues to shape Slovakia's identity today.

The Slovak National Awakening

The Slovak National Awakening, a pivotal chapter in Slovakia's history, marked a period of cultural revival and a renewed sense of national identity. This movement, which unfolded during the 18th and 19th centuries, was a response to centuries of Hungarian rule and cultural assimilation, as well as the broader currents of European nationalism sweeping across the continent.

At the heart of the Slovak National Awakening was the desire to preserve and promote the Slovak language, culture, and heritage. For centuries, Slovaks had been subjected to the dominance of Hungarian culture and the suppression of their own identity. This era saw a resurgence of Slovak pride and the recognition of the importance of preserving their unique linguistic and cultural heritage.

One of the key figures of the Slovak National Awakening was Anton Bernolák, a Catholic priest and linguist. He published the first standardized Slovak language dictionary and grammar, laying the foundation for a unified written Slovak language. His efforts helped establish a common linguistic framework for Slovaks and fostered a sense of linguistic identity.

The awakening also saw the emergence of cultural and educational institutions dedicated to the preservation and promotion of Slovak culture. The establishment of cultural organizations, schools, and publications played a vital role in spreading knowledge of Slovak history, folklore, and literature. This intellectual revival allowed Slovaks to reconnect with their roots and celebrate their cultural heritage.

The 19th century, in particular, witnessed a surge in literary and artistic expression among Slovak intellectuals. Poets like Samo Chalupka and Andrej Sládkovič produced works that celebrated Slovak identity and the beauty of the Slovak landscape. This period also saw the rise of nationalistic literature, which aimed to inspire a sense of pride and patriotism among Slovaks.

The Slovak National Awakening was not without its challenges. It faced resistance from the Hungarian authorities, who sought to suppress any efforts that promoted Slovak identity. Yet, despite these obstacles, the awakening continued to gain momentum, fueled by the determination of Slovak intellectuals and activists.

By the late 19th century, the awakening had made significant strides in fostering a renewed sense of Slovak identity and pride. This newfound sense of nationhood would play a crucial role in the broader political developments of the 20th century, including the eventual establishment of an independent Slovakia in 1993.

In hindsight, the Slovak National Awakening was a pivotal chapter in the nation's history, laying the groundwork for the preservation of the Slovak language, culture, and identity. It served as a beacon of hope and resilience during a time of cultural suppression, and its legacy continues to shape the vibrant and proud nation that is Slovakia today.

Slovakia During World War I and II

The tumultuous years of World War I and II had a profound impact on the history and destiny of Slovakia. Situated in the heart of Europe, Slovakia found itself caught in the crossfire of these global conflicts, with far-reaching consequences for its people and its future.

World War I, which raged from 1914 to 1918, marked the beginning of a new era for Slovakia. At that time, Slovakia was part of the Austro-Hungarian Empire, and many Slovaks were conscripted into the imperial army to fight on the Eastern and Western fronts. The war brought hardships to the civilian population, including food shortages and economic challenges. However, it also ignited a desire for change and autonomy among many Slovaks.

Amid the chaos of World War I, a Czechoslovak independence movement gained momentum. Slovak and Czech leaders, including Tomas Garrigue Masaryk, Edvard Benes, and Milan Rastislav Stefanik, worked tirelessly to secure international recognition for an independent Czechoslovak state. The collapse of the Austro-Hungarian Empire in 1918 created an opportunity for Czechoslovakia to emerge as a new nation, with Slovakia as one of its constituent parts.

The interwar period brought a sense of optimism and newfound freedom for Slovakia. The First Czechoslovak Republic, established in 1918, was a democratic and multi-ethnic state. Slovakia, along with the Czech lands, enjoyed a period of cultural flourishing, economic development, and political stability. However, tensions between the

Czechs and Slovaks simmered beneath the surface, reflecting cultural and linguistic differences.

As the world descended into the darkness of World War II in the late 1930s, Czechoslovakia found itself in a precarious position. In 1938, the Munich Agreement, a diplomatic pact between Nazi Germany, Italy, France, and the United Kingdom, led to the dismemberment of Czechoslovakia. The Sudetenland, a region with a significant ethnic German population, was ceded to Germany without the consent of the Czechoslovak government.

In the wake of the Munich Agreement, Slovakia declared autonomy in 1938, and in 1939, it became a puppet state under the control of Nazi Germany. Jozef Tiso, a Slovak priest, served as the president of this newly-formed Slovak State, which was subservient to Adolf Hitler's Third Reich. This period witnessed the adoption of anti-Semitic policies, leading to the persecution and deportation of Slovak Jews to concentration camps.

World War II further ravaged Slovakia, as it was drawn into the conflict on the side of Nazi Germany. Slovak troops participated in the invasion of Poland in 1939 and later fought on the Eastern Front against the Soviet Union. As the tide of the war turned against the Axis powers, Slovakia faced the consequences of its wartime collaboration with the Nazis.

The end of World War II brought the liberation of Slovakia by Soviet and Allied forces in 1945. Slovakia was subsequently reintegrated into Czechoslovakia, marking the end of its wartime independence.

The Velvet Revolution and Independence

The late 20th century brought monumental changes to Slovakia, culminating in the peaceful Velvet Revolution and the eventual declaration of independence. This transformative period marked the end of decades of communist rule and the beginning of a new chapter in the nation's history.

The Velvet Revolution, which unfolded in Czechoslovakia in late 1989, was a momentous turning point in the country's history. It was a peaceful, nationwide protest against the authoritarian Communist regime that had held power for over four decades. The revolution was sparked by a series of events, including the fall of the Berlin Wall and growing dissatisfaction with the regime's oppressive policies.

Massive demonstrations and strikes erupted across Czechoslovakia, with people from all walks of life demanding political reform, freedom of speech, and democratic elections. The protests were largely non-violent, characterized by their spirit of unity and determination. Key figures, such as Vaclav Havel and Alexander Dubcek, played instrumental roles in galvanizing the movement and advocating for change.

The Communist leadership, under pressure from both internal and international forces, began negotiations with the opposition. In December 1989, Czechoslovak President Gustav Husak appointed a new government that included non-Communist members. This move signaled a significant shift in the political landscape.

The turning point came on December 10, 1989, when President Husak appointed Vaclav Havel, a dissident playwright, as the new President of Czechoslovakia. Havel's presidency marked a symbolic and substantive break from the Communist era. The country began a process of political and economic transformation, transitioning from a one-party system to a multiparty democracy.

In the early 1990s, Czechoslovakia embarked on a path towards the division of the federation into two separate nations: the Czech Republic and Slovakia. The process was peaceful and marked by negotiations, rather than conflict. On January 1, 1993, the two nations officially declared their independence, with Slovakia becoming a sovereign state.

The declaration of independence was a moment of both celebration and reflection for Slovakia. It was a momentous step towards self-determination and the realization of long-held aspirations for independence. Slovakia was now free to shape its own destiny and define its identity on the world stage.

The Velvet Revolution and the subsequent peaceful dissolution of Czechoslovakia demonstrated the power of non-violent protest and the resilience of people in the face of oppression. It paved the way for Slovakia to chart its course as a democratic, sovereign nation, and it set the stage for the challenges and opportunities that would shape its future.

This period of transition, marked by courage, hope, and determination, laid the foundation for the modern Slovakia we know today—a nation with a rich history and a promising future on the global stage.

Government and Political Structure

Slovakia, as a sovereign nation, operates under a democratic parliamentary republic system of government. This political structure has evolved since gaining independence in 1993 and is rooted in democratic principles and the rule of law.

At the heart of Slovakia's political system is the presidency. The President of Slovakia serves as the head of state and plays a ceremonial role in representing the country on the international stage. The president is elected by popular vote for a five-year term and can serve a maximum of two consecutive terms. While the president's powers are largely symbolic, they do include appointing the prime minister, signing bills into law, and representing Slovakia in foreign affairs.

The real political power in Slovakia rests with the government, headed by the Prime Minister. The Prime Minister is the head of government and is responsible for leading the executive branch. They are typically the leader of the political party or coalition that holds the majority in the National Council of the Slovak Republic, the country's legislative body. The Prime Minister appoints cabinet ministers to oversee various government ministries, such as finance, defense, and education.

Slovakia's legislative branch consists of the National Council (Národná rada Slovenskej republiky), a unicameral parliament. The National Council is composed of 150 members who are elected by proportional representation for a four-year term. These members represent the diverse political spectrum of Slovakia and are responsible for passing legislation, approving budgets, and overseeing the government's activities.

The judiciary in Slovakia operates independently and is responsible for upholding the rule of law. The Constitutional Court of Slovakia has the authority to review the constitutionality of laws and government actions. The judiciary includes various levels of courts, with the Supreme Court serving as the highest court in the land.

Slovakia follows a multi-party system, and its political landscape has seen the rise and fall of various political parties and coalitions over the years. The diversity of parties reflects the range of political ideologies and interests present in the country.

Slovakia's political system is anchored in democratic values and is characterized by a commitment to human rights, the protection of civil liberties, and a free-market economy. The country has also been a member of the European Union (EU) since 2004 and the North Atlantic Treaty Organization (NATO) since 2009, further integrating it into the broader European and international political landscape.

The government and political structure in Slovakia have evolved over the years, shaped by historical events, political movements, and the country's transition from communism to democracy. It continues to adapt to the changing needs and aspirations of its citizens, as it navigates the complexities of modern governance in a dynamic global environment.

Economy and Industry

Slovakia's economy has undergone significant transformations since gaining independence in 1993. The country has transitioned from a centrally planned economy, typical of the communist era, to a dynamic and open-market economy that has propelled it into the European Union (EU) and the global economic arena.

One of the key drivers of Slovakia's economic growth has been its strategic location in the heart of Europe. This geographical advantage has made Slovakia an attractive destination for foreign investment and trade. The country shares borders with several EU member states, including Austria, the Czech Republic, and Hungary, providing easy access to these markets.

The automotive industry has emerged as a cornerstone of Slovakia's economy. Leading global car manufacturers, such as Volkswagen, Kia, and Peugeot, have established production facilities in the country. This has not only created thousands of jobs but has also stimulated growth in related industries, including automotive suppliers and logistics.

Slovakia's skilled labor force, relatively low labor costs compared to Western Europe, and a business-friendly environment have contributed to its attractiveness to foreign investors. The country's membership in the EU has also facilitated trade and investment flows, providing businesses with access to a market of over 500 million consumers.

In addition to the automotive sector, Slovakia has a diverse industrial base that includes machinery and equipment production, electronics, and the chemical industry. These sectors have played a crucial role in driving economic growth and export revenues.

The banking and financial services sector in Slovakia has evolved to meet the needs of a modern economy. A stable banking system, along with the adoption of the euro currency in 2009, has promoted economic stability and facilitated international trade and investment.

Slovakia has also made strides in promoting innovation and research and development (R&D). Government initiatives and EU funding have supported innovation-driven growth, and the country is gradually becoming a hub for technology and innovation startups.

The agriculture sector in Slovakia remains significant, although its contribution to the overall economy has decreased over the years. The country is known for its fertile land, and agriculture continues to be an important source of employment, particularly in rural areas.

Despite the economic progress, Slovakia faces challenges, including income inequality and regional disparities. Efforts to address these issues and promote inclusive growth are ongoing. The government has implemented social policies and infrastructure development projects to reduce regional disparities and improve living conditions in economically disadvantaged areas.

In conclusion, Slovakia's economy has come a long way since its days as part of the communist bloc. Its strategic location, skilled workforce, and diverse industrial base have propelled it into the ranks of advanced economies. The country's commitment to economic openness and innovation positions it well for continued growth and development in the global marketplace.

Education and Healthcare System

Slovakia places a strong emphasis on education and healthcare, recognizing them as vital pillars for the well-being and development of its citizens. The country has made significant strides in both sectors since gaining independence in 1993, aligning its systems with European standards and modernizing them to meet the evolving needs of its population.

Education in Slovakia is compulsory for children between the ages of 6 and 16. The education system is divided into several levels: primary education, which lasts for four years, followed by eight years of secondary education. Secondary education branches into general, vocational, or technical tracks, allowing students to pursue academic or practical skills based on their interests and abilities. One notable feature of Slovakia's education system is its strong emphasis on foreign language learning, with English being a widely taught language. The country recognizes the importance of linguistic proficiency in a globalized world and strives to equip its students with valuable language skills.

Higher education in Slovakia is offered at universities and colleges, with a growing number of programs available in English to attract international students. The country boasts several reputable universities, including Comenius University in Bratislava and the Slovak University of Technology in Trnava, known for their contributions to research and innovation. Slovakia places a premium on accessible healthcare for its citizens. The country has a universal healthcare system, with healthcare services funded through a combination of mandatory health insurance contributions, government subsidies, and out-of-pocket payments. Citizens have access to a wide range of medical services, including primary care, specialist care, and hospital services.

Health outcomes in Slovakia have improved over the years, with a focus on preventive care and early diagnosis. The country has also invested in modernizing its healthcare infrastructure and expanding access to medical technologies. This commitment to healthcare has led to increased life expectancy and reduced mortality rates for various diseases.

Pharmaceuticals and medications are an integral part of healthcare in Slovakia, with a well-regulated pharmaceutical industry ensuring the availability of essential drugs. The country has a system in place to control drug prices and promote the use of cost-effective treatments.

Slovakia's healthcare system is characterized by a high degree of professionalism among its healthcare workforce. Physicians and medical professionals receive comprehensive training and are subject to strict licensing and accreditation requirements to ensure the quality of care.

In recent years, Slovakia has also focused on improving mental healthcare services and addressing mental health challenges among its population. Initiatives to reduce stigma surrounding mental health issues and expand access to mental healthcare have been prominent features of the country's healthcare policies.

In conclusion, Slovakia has made significant progress in both education and healthcare since becoming an independent nation. The emphasis on education and the development of a comprehensive healthcare system reflects the government's commitment to the well-being and prosperity of its citizens. These systems continue to evolve and adapt to meet the changing needs and challenges of the 21st century.

Slovak Cuisine: A Culinary Journey

Slovak cuisine is a delightful and hearty reflection of the nation's rich history, diverse regional influences, and the abundance of natural ingredients found in its landscapes. As you embark on a culinary journey through Slovakia, you'll discover a tapestry of flavors, recipes passed down through generations, and a deep connection to tradition and local produce.

One of the defining features of Slovak cuisine is its emphasis on simplicity and reliance on fresh, locally sourced ingredients. The country's fertile land, characterized by rolling plains and fertile valleys, provides an ideal environment for agriculture. Potatoes, cabbage, and wheat are staples in Slovak cuisine, and you'll encounter them in various forms throughout your gastronomic exploration.

A quintessential Slovak dish is "bryndzové halušky," often considered the national dish. It consists of potato dumplings (halušky) smothered in a creamy sheep cheese sauce (bryndza) and topped with bacon. This comforting and savory dish captures the essence of Slovak cuisine.

Meat also plays a prominent role in Slovak cooking, with pork being the most commonly consumed meat. Slovak households take pride in preparing and preserving their own meats, including sausages and smoked hams. You'll find these meats featured in dishes like "kapustnica," a hearty sauerkraut soup with smoked sausage, and "paprikaš," a stew made with various meats and paprika.

Speaking of paprika, this spice is a beloved and essential ingredient in Slovak cuisine. It adds depth and flavor to many dishes, including "goulash" and "paprikáš." Slovak paprika is renowned for its quality and contributes to the rich and aromatic character of the cuisine. Slovakia's natural landscapes also provide an abundance of fresh dairy products, including cheeses and dairy desserts. Aside from bryndza, "tvaroh" (a type of curd cheese) is widely used in sweet and savory dishes. "Parenica," a traditional Slovak cheese, is known for its distinctive smoked flavor and stringy texture.

Bread is another dietary staple in Slovakia, with various types of bread available, from crusty baguettes to hearty rye loaves. Bread is served with nearly every meal and is often used to make open-faced sandwiches or "chlebíčky."

Slovakia's culinary traditions are closely tied to its seasonal rhythms. In the spring, you'll find dishes featuring fresh herbs, asparagus, and young greens. Summer brings an abundance of fruits, berries, and vegetables, while autumn is a time for harvesting mushrooms and preparing hearty stews. Winter sees the emergence of warming and comforting dishes like "kyslá polievka," a sour cabbage soup.

Slovak desserts are a sweet conclusion to any meal. "Palacinky" are thin pancakes often filled with jam or cottage cheese, while "buchty" are sweet yeast dumplings stuffed with fruit or poppy seeds. A favorite holiday treat is "medovník," a honey cake layered with a creamy filling.

The Slovak culinary landscape is also influenced by neighboring countries, including Hungary, Austria, and the Czech Republic, resulting in a diverse and flavorful array of dishes. As you savor the flavors of Slovakia, you'll discover a cuisine deeply rooted in tradition, yet open to innovation and adaptation, reflecting the country's evolving identity in the modern world.

Wildlife and Natural Wonders

Slovakia's diverse and stunning natural landscapes offer a haven for a wide variety of wildlife and showcase an array of breathtaking natural wonders. From dense forests and rugged mountains to pristine lakes and meandering rivers, Slovakia's natural beauty captivates and inspires all who venture into its wilderness. One of the most iconic natural wonders in Slovakia is the High Tatras, a majestic mountain range located in the northern part of the country. The High Tatras are a part of the Carpathian Mountains and boast some of the highest peaks in Central Europe, including Gerlachovský štít, which stands as the tallest peak in Slovakia. These mountains are a paradise for hikers, climbers, and nature enthusiasts, offering breathtaking vistas, alpine lakes, and an opportunity to witness the unique flora and fauna of this high-altitude environment.

Slovakia's rich biodiversity is evident in its national parks and protected areas. The Tatra National Park, which encompasses the High Tatras, is a UNESCO Biosphere Reserve, home to numerous species of plants and animals, including the elusive chamois and the endangered Tatra chamois. The national park also harbors pristine alpine lakes, such as Štrbské pleso and Popradské pleso, which reflect the towering peaks of the Tatras. Beyond the Tatras, Slovakia boasts other remarkable natural wonders. The Slovak Paradise National Park is famous for its deep canyons, gorges, and limestone formations, which make it a paradise for hikers and outdoor enthusiasts. The picturesque Suchá Belá Gorge, with its wooden walkways and waterfalls, is a testament to the natural beauty found in this park. The Demänovská Cave System, located in the Low Tatras, is another remarkable natural wonder. It comprises several interconnected caves, with the Demänovská Ice Cave and Demänovská Cave of Liberty being the most famous. These subterranean marvels offer a glimpse into the mysterious underground world, with stunning stalactite and stalagmite formations.

Slovakia's rivers and lakes also play a vital role in its natural beauty. The Dunajec River, which flows through the Pieniny National Park, offers thrilling rafting adventures through scenic canyons. The Orava River winds its way through the picturesque Orava region, with the Orava Castle perched on a hill overlooking its waters.

Forests cover a significant portion of Slovakia, making up nearly 40% of the country's land area. The vast woodlands are home to a rich variety of wildlife, including brown bears, lynx, wolves, and a multitude of bird species. Protected areas like the Poloniny National Park in the eastern part of Slovakia provide a safe haven for these creatures, as well as pristine beech forests that are part of the UNESCO World Heritage.

Slovakia's natural wonders are not limited to its mountains and forests. The Slovak Karst, another UNESCO World Heritage site, is renowned for its distinctive karst landscapes, sinkholes, and caves. The Domica Cave, part of this karst region, offers visitors a unique underground experience, with chambers adorned with stalactites and an underground river.

The diversity and beauty of Slovakia's wildlife and natural wonders make it a destination for nature lovers and adventurers alike. Whether you're exploring the untamed wilderness of the High Tatras, traversing the winding canyons of Slovak Paradise, or delving into the depths of the Demänovská Caves, Slovakia's natural treasures leave an indelible mark on all who have the privilege to witness them.

Environmental Conservation Efforts

Slovakia has demonstrated a growing commitment to environmental conservation over the years, recognizing the importance of protecting its natural heritage for future generations and contributing to global efforts to address environmental challenges.

One of the key aspects of Slovakia's environmental conservation efforts is its focus on preserving its rich biodiversity. The country's diverse landscapes, including mountains, forests, wetlands, and rivers, provide a habitat for a wide range of plant and animal species. Slovakia has designated numerous protected areas, national parks, and nature reserves to safeguard its natural treasures. These areas serve as sanctuaries for endangered species such as the European brown bear, the Eurasian lynx, and the imperial eagle.

The Carpathian Mountains, including the High Tatras, are part of the larger Carpathian ecoregion, which spans several countries in Central and Eastern Europe. Slovakia actively participates in transnational conservation initiatives to protect the Carpathians' unique ecosystems and wildlife corridors, allowing species to migrate freely across borders. Slovakia's rivers and water bodies are also the focus of conservation efforts. The country is home to various aquatic species, including the Danube salmon and the European otter. Conservation initiatives aim to preserve the ecological health of these waterways and ensure the long-term survival of aquatic life. Efforts to combat air pollution and reduce greenhouse gas emissions have gained momentum in Slovakia. The country has adopted policies to promote renewable energy sources, energy efficiency, and sustainable transportation. The transition to cleaner and more environmentally friendly technologies is a priority, aligning Slovakia with international commitments to address climate change.

Waste management and recycling programs have been established to minimize the environmental impact of waste disposal. Slovakia strives to reduce landfill waste and increase recycling rates, contributing to the conservation of natural resources and the reduction of pollution.

Slovakia's commitment to conservation extends to its participation in international agreements and conventions. The country is a signatory to the Convention on Biological Diversity and the Ramsar Convention on Wetlands, among others. These agreements facilitate cooperation with other nations and provide a framework for shared conservation goals.

Efforts to raise environmental awareness and education are also prominent in Slovakia. Environmental organizations, educational institutions, and government agencies collaborate to inform the public about the importance of conservation and sustainable practices. Initiatives such as reforestation campaigns, wildlife protection programs, and eco-tourism opportunities allow citizens and visitors to engage directly in conservation efforts.

In recent years, Slovakia has faced challenges related to land use changes, urbanization, and infrastructure development. Balancing economic growth with environmental preservation is an ongoing endeavor, and the country continues to refine its policies and strategies to ensure a sustainable future.

Slovak Folklore and Traditions

Slovakia's rich tapestry of folklore and traditions is a testament to the nation's cultural heritage, spanning centuries of history and reflecting the influences of various ethnic groups that have called this land home. These cherished customs and practices provide a glimpse into the soul of Slovakia, celebrating its resilience, identity, and the enduring spirit of its people. One of the most celebrated elements of Slovak folklore is its traditional music. Folk music in Slovakia varies from region to region, with distinctive styles and instruments. The fujara, a long shepherd's flute, and the violin are integral to Slovak folk music. Traditional songs and dances, such as the "Čardáš" and "Horehronský Čardáš," are often performed at festivals, weddings, and other social gatherings. These lively and spirited performances are a source of national pride and a way to connect with the past.

Slovakia's rich oral tradition is another cornerstone of its folklore. Folk tales, legends, and myths have been passed down through generations, recounting stories of heroes, magical creatures, and the struggles of everyday life. The character of Juraj Jánošík, a legendary Slovak outlaw, remains a prominent figure in Slovak folklore, symbolizing the spirit of rebellion against oppression. The Slovak language itself is a reflection of the country's cultural identity and traditions. Slovak is a Slavic language with a distinct vocabulary, grammar, and pronunciation. The preservation and promotion of the Slovak language are central to preserving the nation's cultural heritage. Traditional craftsmanship and handiwork are also deeply ingrained in Slovak culture. Slovak artisans are known for their skills in pottery, woodcarving, embroidery, and the creation of intricate folk costumes. Each region in Slovakia has its own distinct costume, often adorned with vibrant colors and intricate patterns. These costumes are proudly worn during special occasions and cultural festivals, preserving a connection to the past.

Slovak cuisine is steeped in tradition and reflects the country's agrarian history. Meals are often based on simple, locally sourced ingredients. Specialties like "halušky" (potato dumplings) and "pierogi" (dumplings filled with various ingredients) are cherished comfort foods. Many traditional dishes are prepared for festive occasions and holidays, such as "kapustnica" (sauerkraut soup) for Christmas and "paska" (a sweet Easter bread) for Easter.

Religious traditions play a significant role in Slovak culture. Christianity, particularly Catholicism, has had a profound influence on the country's customs and celebrations. Religious festivals, such as Christmas and Easter, are observed with reverence and are accompanied by unique rituals and ceremonies.

Slovakia's calendar is filled with a myriad of folk festivals and celebrations, each with its own unique traditions. The "Obchodníci" in St. Nicholas costumes and the "Krampus" figures during the Christmas season are just a few examples of the colorful characters that make appearances during these festivities.

Slovakia's folklore and traditions are not static but continue to evolve in response to contemporary influences and changing times. Nevertheless, they remain an essential part of the country's cultural identity, providing a connection to its past and a source of pride for its people. Whether through music, stories, costumes, or cuisine, Slovakia's rich folklore and traditions offer a window into its soul, revealing the enduring spirit and resilience of a nation with a vibrant cultural heritage.

Festivals and Celebrations

Slovakia is a land of vibrant festivals and celebrations that reflect the country's rich cultural diversity and deep-rooted traditions. These lively and colorful events provide a window into the heart and soul of Slovak life, offering a glimpse of the nation's history, folklore, and the enduring spirit of its people.

One of the most eagerly anticipated celebrations in Slovakia is Easter, a significant religious holiday marked by a range of customs and traditions. The Easter season begins with "Fasiangy," a pre-Lenten carnival filled with masks, costumes, and lively processions. It culminates in the "Veľká Noc" (Great Night), where families gather to share a traditional Easter meal and exchange beautifully decorated eggs. The Easter Monday tradition of "šibačka," where boys gently whip girls with decorated willow branches in exchange for eggs or gifts, adds a playful element to the holiday.

Christmas is another cherished time of year in Slovakia, marked by a month-long Advent period filled with festive markets, concerts, and nativity scenes. The holiday itself is celebrated with a rich array of traditions, including the Midnight Mass, the lighting of the Christmas tree, and the placement of hay under the tablecloth to symbolize the stable in Bethlehem. On Christmas Eve, families come together to share a meatless meal, often featuring "kapustnica" (sauerkraut soup) and "lokše" (potato pancakes).

Slovakia's unique folklore and traditions come alive during various festivals throughout the year. The "Cabbage Festival" in the village of Bátovce celebrates the importance of cabbage in Slovak cuisine, while the "Pipe Festival" in the town of Detva showcases the traditional craftsmanship of pipe-making. The "Kraslice Festival" highlights the art of egg decorating, a skill passed down through generations.

Music plays a central role in Slovakia's cultural celebrations. The "Folklore Festival Východná" features vibrant folk music and dance performances from different regions of the country. The "Budatín Castle Music Festival" showcases classical music in a historic setting, and the "Bratislava Music Festival" attracts renowned international musicians.

Slovakia's diverse ethnic communities also contribute to the nation's tapestry of festivals. The Roma culture is celebrated during the "Gypsy Fest" in the town of Sabinov, featuring Roma music, dance, and cuisine. The "Ukrainian Days" festival in Snina showcases Ukrainian traditions, and the "Hungarian Cultural Summer" in Komárno celebrates Hungarian heritage.

The wine regions of Slovakia come alive during wine festivals, where visitors can taste a variety of Slovak wines, learn about winemaking, and enjoy local cuisine. The "Víno na hrade" (Wine at the Castle) festival held in various castle settings is a highlight for wine enthusiasts.

Slovakia's calendar is also marked by national holidays such as Constitution Day, Liberation Day, and Independence Day, which are celebrated with parades, patriotic events, and historical reenactments.

Throughout the year, Slovakia's festivals and celebrations serve as a testament to the country's cultural diversity and enduring traditions. They provide opportunities for both locals and visitors to connect with the heart and soul of this dynamic and culturally rich nation, where the past and present converge in a joyful and vibrant celebration of life.

Slovak Music and Dance

Slovak music and dance are vibrant expressions of the country's cultural identity, reflecting its rich history, diverse regional influences, and the enduring spirit of its people. These art forms serve as a dynamic link to Slovakia's past and continue to evolve in contemporary contexts, celebrating both tradition and innovation.

Folk music holds a special place in Slovak culture, and it is deeply intertwined with the nation's history and everyday life. The melodies and rhythms of Slovak folk songs vary from region to region, each with its distinctive style and instruments. The fujara, a long wooden flute, and the violin are iconic instruments often used in folk music performances. Songs and dances are integral to celebrations, festivals, and social gatherings, adding a lively and spirited dimension to Slovak culture.

One of the most beloved folk dances in Slovakia is the "Čardáš," known for its lively tempo, intricate footwork, and colorful costumes. Dancers often perform the Čardáš at weddings and other festive occasions, creating an atmosphere of joy and celebration. Another popular dance is the "Krútivý tanec," characterized by graceful spins and intricate partner choreography.

Slovakia's folklore is rich in storytelling, and folk songs often convey tales of love, nature, and historical events. The lyrical beauty of these songs, often accompanied by heartfelt vocals, captures the essence of Slovak life and emotions. Traditional instruments, including the shepherd's flute and bagpipes, add a distinctive flavor to folk music performances. In addition to folk music, classical music has a significant presence in Slovakia's cultural landscape. Composers such as Johann Nepomuk Hummel, Eugen Suchoň, and Béla Bartók have made significant contributions to the world of classical music. The country boasts several renowned orchestras and opera companies that perform both classical and contemporary works.

Slovakia has a thriving contemporary music scene, with artists spanning various genres, including pop, rock, hip-hop, and electronic music. Many Slovak musicians have achieved international recognition, and the country hosts music festivals that showcase local talent and international acts. The "Pohoda Festival" is one of the largest and most diverse music festivals in Slovakia, attracting a diverse range of artists and music enthusiasts from around the world.

Dance also plays a crucial role in contemporary Slovak culture. Modern dance companies and traditional dance ensembles perform throughout the country and abroad, preserving and reimagining Slovak dance traditions. Slovak dancers have earned acclaim in various dance styles, including ballet, contemporary dance, and folk-inspired choreography.

Slovak music and dance continue to evolve and adapt to contemporary influences while preserving their deep-rooted traditions. The fusion of old and new, traditional and innovative, reflects the country's dynamic cultural identity. Through music and dance, Slovakia celebrates its past, embraces its present, and looks toward a future where the arts remain a vibrant and integral part of its cultural heritage.

Visual Arts and Contemporary Culture

Slovakia's visual arts and contemporary culture provide a fascinating glimpse into the nation's creative spirit, reflecting its history, identity, and the evolving trends of the modern world. From traditional craftsmanship to contemporary art forms, Slovakia's cultural landscape is a dynamic fusion of tradition and innovation.

Traditional Slovak craftsmanship has deep roots in the country's history. The art of pottery, woodcarving, and textile production has been passed down through generations, preserving the techniques and aesthetics of the past. Skilled artisans create intricate pottery, beautifully carved wooden sculptures, and exquisite textiles, all of which contribute to Slovakia's rich cultural heritage.

One of the most celebrated forms of Slovak visual art is the craft of "fujara" making. The fujara, a long wooden flute with a distinctive three-hole mouthpiece, is not only a musical instrument but also a work of art. These intricately crafted instruments often feature detailed carvings and decorative elements, making them both functional and visually stunning. Fujara-making is recognized as an important cultural tradition and has been inscribed on the UNESCO Representative List of the Intangible Cultural Heritage of Humanity.

Contemporary Slovak art has also flourished in the modern era, with artists exploring a wide range of styles and mediums. Slovak painters, sculptors, and photographers have gained recognition on the international stage, pushing the boundaries of artistic expression. Their works often reflect the country's history, landscape, and contemporary concerns, offering unique perspectives on Slovak culture and society.

The Slovak art scene includes a diverse array of galleries, museums, and exhibition spaces that showcase the work of both emerging and established artists. The Slovak National Gallery in Bratislava is one of the country's foremost institutions dedicated to visual arts, housing an extensive collection of Slovak and international artworks. The Andy Warhol Museum of Modern Art in Medzilaborce pays homage to the iconic pop artist, who had Slovak roots.

Slovakia's contemporary culture extends beyond the visual arts to include literature, film, theater, and design. Slovak literature has a rich tradition, with notable authors such as Milan Kundera, whose work has gained international acclaim. Slovak cinema has also made its mark on the global stage, with films like "The Shop on Main Street" winning the Academy Award for Best Foreign Language Film.

Theater and performing arts are vibrant in Slovakia, with a thriving theater scene that encompasses both traditional and experimental productions. The country hosts numerous theater festivals and events throughout the year, attracting theater enthusiasts and artists from around the world.

Slovakia's contemporary culture also embraces design and architecture. Modern architectural projects blend seamlessly with historic structures, creating a unique urban landscape. The country's designers and architects have contributed to innovative projects that redefine spaces and reflect the evolving needs of society.

In conclusion, Slovakia's visual arts and contemporary culture are a testament to the nation's creative vitality and its ability to adapt and thrive in a rapidly changing world. From traditional craftsmanship to cutting-edge artistic expressions, Slovakia's cultural landscape is a dynamic fusion of tradition and innovation, offering a window into the vibrant and evolving spirit of the nation.

Slovak Literature and Writers

Slovak literature is a rich tapestry of storytelling, poetry, and prose that reflects the nation's history, culture, and the enduring spirit of its people. The Slovak literary tradition has deep roots, and its writers have made significant contributions to world literature. From early folk tales to contemporary novels, Slovak literature offers a captivating journey through time and imagination.

The origins of Slovak literature can be traced back to the Middle Ages when Latin was the dominant language of written expression. Religious texts, chronicles, and early Slovak manuscripts written in Latin provide insights into the intellectual and cultural life of the time. One of the earliest known Slovak literary works is the "Nitra Gospels," a Latin manuscript dating back to the 11th century.

As the Slovak language began to emerge as a literary medium, so did a rich tradition of folk tales and oral storytelling. These narratives, passed down through generations, explored themes of folklore, morality, and the human experience. Characters like Juraj Jánošík, a legendary Slovak outlaw, and fairytale figures such as Janko Hraško continue to captivate readers of all ages.

The 19th century marked a significant period in Slovak literature, often referred to as the Slovak National Awakening. Writers and poets, including Samo Chalupka and Ján Kollár, played pivotal roles in promoting Slovak identity and language. Their works celebrated Slovak culture, history, and the beauty of the Slovak landscape, igniting a cultural revival that laid the foundation for modern Slovak literature.

One of the most influential figures in Slovak literature is Pavol Országh Hviezdoslav, a prolific poet and playwright. His lyrical and evocative poetry explored themes of love, nature, and the human condition, earning him acclaim as one of Slovakia's greatest literary treasures. His poetic legacy continues to inspire generations of Slovak writers and readers.

The 20th century witnessed a flourishing of Slovak literature, with writers like Martin Rázus, Milo Urban, and Dominik Tatarka making their mark. Their works grappled with the complexities of modernity, societal changes, and the impact of historical events such as World War II and the Communist era. These authors contributed to a diverse literary landscape that encompassed poetry, prose, drama, and critical essays.

In the realm of contemporary literature, Slovak authors have continued to produce acclaimed works that resonate with readers both at home and abroad. Renowned writers like Pavel Vilikovský, Dušan Dušek, and Jana Beňová have explored themes of identity, globalization, and the human experience in a rapidly changing world. Their novels and stories have earned recognition on the international stage, bringing Slovak literature to a global audience.

Slovak literature today thrives in a digital age, with writers and poets sharing their works through various platforms, including social media and online publications. The literary scene remains vibrant, with literary festivals, book fairs, and creative writing workshops fostering a community of aspiring writers and avid readers.

In conclusion, Slovak literature is a testament to the enduring power of words and storytelling. From its humble beginnings in folk tales and Latin manuscripts to the complex and diverse narratives of contemporary authors, Slovak literature continues to evolve, enriching the cultural heritage of Slovakia and offering a window into the hearts and minds of its people.

Religion in Slovakia

Religion in Slovakia is a deeply ingrained and diverse aspect of the nation's identity and culture. Over the centuries, Slovakia has been influenced by various religious traditions, each leaving its mark on the country's spiritual landscape. From Christianity to Judaism and beyond, religion in Slovakia is a complex tapestry that reflects the nation's historical, social, and religious diversity.

Christianity, specifically Catholicism, has played a significant role in shaping the religious landscape of Slovakia. The majority of Slovaks identify as Roman Catholics, and the Catholic Church has been a central institution in the country's history. The arrival of Christianity in the early medieval period marked a transformative moment, as churches and monasteries were established, becoming centers of education, culture, and spirituality. The Vatican played a crucial role in the spread of Christianity in the region, and today, the Catholic Church continues to hold a prominent place in Slovak society.

In addition to Roman Catholicism, Slovakia is home to various Christian denominations, including Greek Catholicism, Evangelical Lutheranism, and Reformed Christianity. Each denomination has its own religious practices, traditions, and followers, contributing to the country's religious diversity. The Eastern Orthodox Church also has a presence in Slovakia, particularly among the Rusyn minority in the eastern part of the country. The Rusyns have a unique religious and cultural heritage, influenced by Orthodox Christianity and the traditions of the Carpathian region. Slovakia has a rich Jewish history dating back to the Middle Ages. Jewish communities established synagogues, schools, and cultural institutions in various Slovak towns and cities. However, the Holocaust during World War II had a devastating impact on Slovakia's Jewish population, with many deported and killed. Today, there are efforts to preserve and commemorate the Jewish heritage of the country, with synagogues and Jewish museums serving as important cultural and historical landmarks.

Islam has a presence in Slovakia, primarily among the Tatar community, whose ancestors settled in the region centuries ago. While the Muslim population is relatively small, the community has maintained its religious practices and traditions.

Slovakia is also home to smaller religious communities, including Buddhists, Hindus, and adherents of various new religious movements. These communities contribute to the country's religious diversity and cultural fabric.

In recent years, secularism and non-religious identities have been on the rise in Slovakia, particularly among younger generations. While religious practices and beliefs remain important to many, there is also a growing trend of secularization and a shift away from traditional religious institutions.

Religion in Slovakia is not only a matter of faith but also an integral part of the country's cultural heritage. Religious festivals, celebrations, and traditions continue to play a significant role in Slovak life, providing opportunities for communities to come together and celebrate their shared beliefs and values.

Architecture and Landmarks

Slovakia's architecture and landmarks tell a captivating story of its history, culture, and evolving identity. From ancient castles perched on rugged hills to modern architectural marvels in bustling cities, the country's architectural heritage is a testament to its rich and diverse past.

One of the most iconic architectural features of Slovakia is its medieval castles and fortresses. These imposing structures, often nestled in picturesque landscapes, reflect the country's historical significance as a crossroads of trade and culture. The Spiš Castle, a UNESCO World Heritage Site, is one of the largest medieval fortresses in Europe and stands as a testament to the architectural prowess of the time. Other notable castles, such as the Bojnice Castle with its romantic architecture and Orava Castle set against a dramatic mountain backdrop, continue to enchant visitors with their timeless charm.

Slovakia is also known for its well-preserved historic towns and villages, where centuries-old architecture transports visitors back in time. The medieval town of Bardejov, another UNESCO World Heritage Site, boasts a beautifully preserved town center with charming Gothic and Renaissance buildings. The town of Levoča is renowned for its stunning St. James's Church, featuring the tallest wooden altar in the world.

The capital city, Bratislava, showcases a mix of architectural styles, reflecting its history as the coronation city of Hungarian kings. The Bratislava Castle, perched on a hill overlooking the city, is a striking example of medieval fortress architecture. In contrast, the Blue Church, an Art Nouveau gem, stands out with its distinctive blue facade and intricate detailing. Modern architecture has also made its mark in Slovakia's urban centers. The UFO Bridge in Bratislava, with its futuristic design and panoramic views, has become an iconic symbol of the city. The Slovak Radio Building, a striking example of functionalist architecture, showcases the country's commitment to modern design.

Religious architecture is another highlight of Slovakia's architectural landscape. The St. Martin's Cathedral in Bratislava, where Hungarian kings were crowned, is a stunning example of Gothic architecture. The wooden churches of the Carpathian region, such as the Church of St. Nicholas in Bodružal, are unique and charming, showcasing the craftsmanship of local artisans.

Slovakia's architectural heritage is not limited to buildings alone. The country is home to natural landmarks of breathtaking beauty, such as the High Tatras, a mountain range with rugged peaks and pristine lakes. The Dobsinska Ice Cave, a UNESCO World Heritage Site, is a mesmerizing underground wonder with stunning ice formations.

In recent years, Slovakia has embraced contemporary architecture, with innovative designs shaping its cityscapes. The Slovak National Theater in Bratislava, with its sleek and modern facade, is a prominent example of this trend.

In conclusion, Slovakia's architecture and landmarks form a captivating tapestry that weaves together the threads of history, culture, and modernity. From medieval castles to modern skyscrapers, from charming historic towns to pristine natural wonders, Slovakia's architectural heritage is a reflection of its diverse and evolving identity, inviting visitors to explore its rich history and cultural legacy.

Bratislava: The Capital City

Nestled along the banks of the mighty Danube River, Bratislava, the capital city of Slovakia, is a vibrant and historically rich European metropolis. With a history dating back centuries, Bratislava has been a witness to the rise and fall of empires, the coronation of kings, and the winds of change that have shaped modern Slovakia.

As one of Europe's smaller capitals, Bratislava exudes an intimate and inviting charm. The city's historic core, with its well-preserved architecture and cobblestone streets, invites visitors to wander through its past. Bratislava's Old Town is a treasure trove of Gothic, Renaissance, Baroque, and Art Nouveau buildings, showcasing the architectural legacy of its diverse history.

One of the city's most iconic landmarks is the Bratislava Castle, perched majestically on a hill overlooking the Danube. This imposing fortress has witnessed centuries of history and offers panoramic views of the city and the surrounding countryside. Inside the castle, visitors can explore exhibitions that delve into the city's past and the role it has played in shaping Slovakia's identity. St. Martin's Cathedral, with its soaring Gothic spire, is another significant architectural gem in Bratislava. This cathedral holds historical importance as the coronation site of Hungarian kings, and its interior features intricate stonework and stunning stained glass windows.

Bratislava's unique blend of architectural styles is evident as you stroll through the city. The Primate's Palace, a neoclassical masterpiece, is known for its exquisite Hall of Mirrors where the Treaty of Pressburg, ending the War of the Third Coalition, was signed in 1805. In contrast, the Blue

Church, or St. Elizabeth's Church, stands out with its vibrant blue facade and Art Nouveau design. The city's squares, such as Hlavné námestie (Main Square) and Hviezdoslavovo námestie, are lively hubs filled with cafes, restaurants, and cultural events. The lively atmosphere, especially during the summer months, draws both locals and tourists alike.

Bratislava's modern side is equally intriguing. The UFO Bridge, named for its distinctive shape, offers breathtaking views from its observation deck. The Danube River promenade, lined with cafes and parks, provides a picturesque setting for leisurely walks.

Cultural life thrives in Bratislava, with a wealth of museums, galleries, and theaters. The Slovak National Theater, with its stunning neo-Renaissance building, hosts opera, ballet, and drama performances. The city's museums cover a wide range of topics, from Slovak history and art to music and natural history.

For those with a penchant for culinary exploration, Bratislava's dining scene is a delightful surprise. Traditional Slovak dishes, such as bryndzové halušky (potato dumplings with sheep cheese) and kapustnica (sauerkraut soup), can be savored alongside international cuisines in the city's restaurants and cafes.

In conclusion, Bratislava, the capital of Slovakia, is a city that seamlessly blends its rich historical heritage with a dynamic modern spirit. Its architecture, cultural offerings, and picturesque surroundings make it a captivating destination for travelers seeking to discover the heart and soul of Slovakia's capital city. Bratislava's charm lies in its ability to reveal the layers of history that have shaped it, all while embracing the contemporary influences that make it a thriving European capital.

Kosice: Slovakia's Second Largest City

Kosice, located in the eastern part of Slovakia, proudly holds the title of the country's second-largest city and serves as a dynamic cultural, historical, and economic hub. With a rich history that spans centuries and a contemporary vibrancy that keeps pace with the modern world, Kosice is a captivating destination that offers a glimpse into the heart of Slovakia's eastern region.

One of the most striking features of Kosice is its well-preserved historic center, a testament to the city's storied past. The Main Street (Hlavná ulica) is a charming pedestrian thoroughfare flanked by picturesque buildings that showcase a blend of architectural styles, including Gothic, Renaissance, and Baroque. The city's impressive St. Elisabeth Cathedral, a dominant Gothic masterpiece, graces the Main Street and is known for its soaring spire and captivating interior.

Kosice's history is closely intertwined with its role as a bustling medieval trading post. Its strategic location along trade routes brought prosperity, and the city was granted numerous privileges by Hungarian kings, further enhancing its significance. One such privilege was the granting of the first town coat of arms in Europe in 1369, which is proudly displayed on the façade of the historical Golden Royal House.

The city's cultural scene is vibrant and diverse, with numerous museums, galleries, and theaters. The East Slovak Museum houses an extensive collection that spans the fields of archaeology, history, and fine arts, offering insights into the region's past and cultural heritage. The Slovak State Philharmonic, located in the majestic House of Arts, hosts classical music concerts that enchant both residents and visitors. Kosice's lively atmosphere extends to its annual cultural events, including the International Peace Marathon, which has been held since 1924 and is one of the oldest marathons in the world. The Kosice Children's Heritage Days, a celebration of Slovak folklore and traditions, provides a colorful and educational experience for families.

The city's modern side is exemplified by its universities, research institutions, and a growing IT sector. Kosice is home to several universities, including the Technical University and the Pavol Jozef Šafárik University, fostering a diverse academic environment. The city's thriving business sector is part of its continuous development, making it an economic center in eastern Slovakia.

Kosice's dining scene offers a delightful blend of traditional Slovak cuisine and international flavors. Visitors can savor local specialties like goulash, halušky (potato dumplings), and tasty pastries in charming restaurants and eateries throughout the city.

Kosice's natural surroundings also beckon outdoor enthusiasts. The nearby High Tatras mountains, part of the Carpathian range, provide opportunities for hiking, skiing, and exploring pristine wilderness.

In conclusion, Kosice, Slovakia's second-largest city, is a captivating blend of history, culture, and modernity. Its well-preserved historic center, rich cultural offerings, and dynamic economic activity make it a significant and inviting destination in eastern Slovakia. Whether you're strolling along the historic streets, admiring architectural marvels, or indulging in local cuisine, Kosice offers a multifaceted experience that reveals the depth and diversity of this remarkable city.

Presov: A Historic Gem

Presov, a city nestled in the heart of eastern Slovakia, stands as a true historic gem that has witnessed centuries of change and continuity. With a rich tapestry of history, culture, and architecture, Presov captivates visitors with its well-preserved heritage and its role as a vibrant center in the region.

The city's origins can be traced back to the 13th century when it was founded by Hungarian King Bela IV. As one of the earliest royal towns in Slovakia, Presov quickly became a vital trade and cultural hub. Its strategic location at the crossroads of trade routes contributed to its prosperity, and the city's history is intertwined with the various rulers and empires that left their mark on this enchanting place.

Presov's Old Town is a testament to its historical significance, featuring a captivating array of architectural styles. The main square, Hlavná ulica, is a picturesque ensemble of colorful facades, quaint cafes, and charming boutiques. The majestic Gothic Cathedral of St. Nicholas dominates the square and serves as a focal point of the city's skyline.

One of the city's iconic landmarks is the wooden Church of St. Paraskeva, a UNESCO World Heritage Site located in the nearby village of Bodružal. This remarkable church, built entirely from wood without the use of nails, is a testament to the craftsmanship of the local people and a unique example of Carpathian wooden architecture.

Presov's history is also marked by its multicultural heritage. Over the centuries, the city was home to various ethnic and religious communities, including Slovaks, Hungarians, Jews, and Ruthenians. This diversity has left a lasting impact on the city's cultural landscape, reflected in its traditions, festivals, and architectural influences.

The city's cultural life is rich and vibrant, with numerous museums, galleries, and theaters. The Presov Museum, housed in a beautiful neoclassical building, showcases the region's history, art, and archaeology. The city's theaters offer a range of performances, from classical drama to contemporary productions, providing entertainment for both residents and visitors.

Presov's location in the eastern part of Slovakia makes it an ideal starting point for exploring the nearby natural wonders. The High Tatras, a stunning mountain range known for its rugged peaks and pristine lakes, are just a short drive away. Nature enthusiasts can embark on hiking adventures, explore caves, and enjoy the breathtaking landscapes that surround the city.

Culinary experiences in Presov are a delightful journey into the flavors of Slovak cuisine. Local dishes, such as bryndzové halušky (potato dumplings with sheep cheese), pirohy (dumplings), and kapustnica (sauerkraut soup), can be savored in traditional restaurants and eateries, providing a taste of authentic Slovak flavors.

In conclusion, Presov, a historic gem in eastern Slovakia, invites visitors to step back in time and immerse themselves in its rich heritage. Its well-preserved architecture, multicultural influences, and cultural offerings make it a city that exudes charm and history at every corner. Whether you're exploring its medieval streets, admiring its architectural treasures, or savoring its local cuisine, Presov offers a captivating experience that celebrates the enduring spirit of this remarkable city.

Banska Bystrica: Heart of Slovakia

Nestled in the heart of Slovakia, Banska Bystrica is a city with a soul that beats to the rhythm of its rich history, diverse culture, and stunning natural surroundings. It holds a special place in the tapestry of Slovak cities, and its story is one of resilience, tradition, and progress.

The city's origins date back to the 13th century when it was established as a mining settlement. The surrounding mountains, particularly the nearby Low Tatras, were abundant in valuable minerals, making Banska Bystrica a center for mining and metallurgy. Its prosperity grew as it became a hub for trade and industry, and its historical significance is evident in its well-preserved architecture.

Banska Bystrica's historic center is a treasure trove of architectural styles, reflecting the city's evolution through the centuries. The Main Square, with its colorful facades and charming cafes, is a picturesque representation of the city's vibrant spirit. Dominating the square is the majestic St. Francis Xavier Cathedral, an impressive Baroque masterpiece that stands as a testament to the city's devotion.

One of the city's most iconic landmarks is the Slovak National Uprising Memorial, perched atop a hill overlooking the city. This monumental complex commemorates the Slovak National Uprising against the Axis powers during World War II. The memorial's imposing monument, surrounded by lush parkland, offers panoramic views of Banska Bystrica and serves as a poignant reminder of the city's role in the fight for freedom. Banska Bystrica's history is marked by its multicultural heritage, where Slovaks, Germans, Hungarians, and other ethnic groups coexisted for centuries. This diversity is reflected in the city's traditions, festivals, and cultural influences, creating a rich tapestry of local identity.

The city's cultural scene is vibrant, with museums, galleries, and theaters that celebrate its heritage and creativity. The Central Slovak Museum, housed in a historic building, offers insights into the region's history, art, and archaeology. Banska Bystrica's theaters showcase a range of performances, from classical drama to contemporary productions, providing cultural enrichment for residents and visitors alike.

Nature enthusiasts will find Banska Bystrica's location ideal for exploration. The nearby Low Tatras National Park offers hiking trails, skiing slopes, and opportunities to immerse oneself in the stunning natural beauty of the region. The Hron River, which flows through the city, provides a tranquil backdrop for leisurely walks and outdoor activities.

Culinary experiences in Banska Bystrica are a delightful journey into Slovak cuisine. Local dishes, such as bryndzové halušky (potato dumplings with sheep cheese), pirohy (dumplings), and traditional pastries, can be savored in cozy restaurants and eateries that showcase the region's culinary traditions.

In conclusion, Banska Bystrica, often referred to as the "Heart of Slovakia," is a city that embodies the essence of the nation. Its history, architecture, culture, and natural surroundings converge to create a unique and captivating destination. Whether you're strolling through its historic streets, admiring its architectural treasures, or exploring the beauty of its surroundings, Banska Bystrica offers an experience that resonates with the heartbeat of this remarkable city and the nation it represents.

Nitra: The Oldest Slovak City

Nitra, with its roots stretching back over a thousand years, holds the esteemed title of being the oldest city in Slovakia. Situated in the southwestern part of the country, it stands as a testament to the enduring history and cultural heritage of the Slovak nation.

The city's origins can be traced to the 9th century when it served as a prominent center of the Great Moravian Empire, one of the earliest Slavic states in Europe. This period marks the dawn of Nitra's historical significance, as it was a crucial political, religious, and cultural hub during that time.

Nitra's most iconic landmark is the Nitra Castle, perched majestically on a hill overlooking the city. This medieval fortress has witnessed centuries of history and has evolved through various architectural styles, from Romanesque to Gothic and Renaissance. It serves as a physical embodiment of the city's historical continuity and has been a symbol of power and governance throughout the ages.

The city's historic center is a captivating blend of architectural styles, reflecting the influences of the many cultures that have called Nitra home over the centuries. The Main Square, with its colorful facades and bustling cafes, exudes a charming atmosphere that invites visitors to wander through its past. St. Emmeram's Cathedral, an exquisite example of Romanesque architecture, graces the square with its elegance.

Nitra's history is closely tied to its role as an ecclesiastical center, and it is often referred to as the "Mother of Slovak Towns." The city played a significant role in the Christianization of the region, with the arrival of Saints Cyril and Methodius in the 9th century, who brought Christianity and the Glagolitic alphabet to the Slavic peoples.

The city's cultural heritage is celebrated through various museums, galleries, and cultural events. The Nitra Gallery showcases a diverse collection of Slovak and international art, providing insights into the region's artistic legacy. The Andrej Bagar Theater, one of Slovakia's oldest theaters, hosts a range of performances, from classical drama to contemporary plays.

Nitra's natural surroundings are characterized by the fertile Nitra Basin, which has played a crucial role in the city's agricultural history. The lush countryside, with its vineyards and orchards, offers a picturesque backdrop for exploring the region's rural charm.

Culinary experiences in Nitra offer a delightful journey into Slovak cuisine. Traditional dishes, such as bryndzové halušky (potato dumplings with sheep cheese) and lokše (potato pancakes), can be savored in local restaurants and eateries, providing a taste of authentic Slovak flavors.

In conclusion, Nitra, the oldest Slovak city, stands as a living testament to the enduring history, culture, and heritage of the Slovak nation. Its rich architectural tapestry, historic significance, and cultural contributions make it a city that resonates with the echoes of the past while embracing the present. Whether you're exploring its medieval streets, admiring its architectural treasures, or savoring its culinary delights, Nitra offers a captivating experience that celebrates the enduring spirit of this remarkable city.

Trnava: City of Saints

Trnava, often referred to as the "City of Saints," is a city in western Slovakia with a history deeply intertwined with religion, culture, and education. Its rich heritage has earned it a reputation as a spiritual and intellectual center, and it stands as a testament to the enduring influence of faith in the region.

The city's roots can be traced back to the 13th century when it was founded as a market town. However, it was in the following centuries that Trnava began to truly flourish, thanks in part to its strategic location along important trade routes and its close ties to the Catholic Church.

One of the most striking features of Trnava is its impressive collection of churches and religious institutions. The city's skyline is adorned with the spires and domes of numerous churches, earning it the nickname "Little Rome." The St. John the Baptist Cathedral, a magnificent example of Gothic and Baroque architecture, stands as the city's dominant religious symbol. Its interior is adorned with exquisite frescoes and sculptures that reflect the city's deep religious devotion.

Trnava has a unique tradition of city fortifications, with well-preserved city walls and gates that harken back to its medieval past. The city's fortifications served not only as a means of defense but also as a testament to the prosperity of the town. Walking along these ancient walls provides a glimpse into Trnava's historical significance. The city's religious heritage is also celebrated through its numerous monasteries and educational institutions. The Trnava

University, founded in the 17th century, was one of the first universities in Central Europe and played a pivotal role in the region's intellectual development. The Jesuit College, with its impressive library, served as a center of learning and culture.

Trnava's devotion to its religious traditions is evident in its annual Corpus Christi procession, a colorful and solemn event that attracts thousands of participants and spectators. This religious procession is a vibrant display of faith and community spirit.

The city's cultural life extends beyond its religious heritage. The Jan Koniarek Gallery, named after a renowned Slovak sculptor, showcases contemporary art and hosts exhibitions that contribute to Slovakia's cultural landscape. The city's theaters offer a range of performances, from classical plays to modern productions, enriching the cultural experience for residents and visitors.

Culinary traditions in Trnava offer a taste of Slovak cuisine, with local specialties like bryndzové halušky (potato dumplings with sheep cheese) and lokše (potato pancakes) gracing the menus of local restaurants and eateries.

In conclusion, Trnava, the "City of Saints," is a place where faith, culture, and history converge. Its religious heritage, impressive architecture, and cultural contributions make it a city that resonates with the echoes of devotion and intellectual pursuit. Whether you're exploring its historic churches, walking along the city walls, or savoring its culinary delights, Trnava offers a unique and enriching experience that celebrates the enduring spirit of this remarkable city.

Martin: Gateway to the Tatras

Nestled in the northern part of Slovakia, Martin serves as a gateway to the spectacular Tatra Mountains, a breathtaking natural wonder that draws nature enthusiasts and adventurers from around the world. With its own unique charm and rich history, Martin is more than just a starting point for exploring the Tatras; it's a destination in its own right.

The city's origins can be traced back to the Middle Ages when it was a market town along the trade routes that crisscrossed the region. Over time, it grew in importance, becoming an administrative center and a hub for culture and education.

Martin is known for its devotion to Slovak culture and heritage. One of its notable institutions is the Slovak National Museum, the oldest museum in Slovakia, founded in 1868. The museum's extensive collections include archaeological artifacts, historical documents, and ethnographic exhibits, providing insights into the country's history and traditions.

The city's historic center exudes a charming atmosphere with its well-preserved buildings and picturesque streets. The Church of St. Martin, a dominant feature of the city's skyline, is a beautiful example of Gothic architecture and serves as a testament to the city's religious heritage.

Martin's cultural scene thrives with theaters, galleries, and cultural events. The Slovak Chamber Theater, one of the country's leading theaters, offers a diverse repertoire of dramatic performances that captivate audiences. The Turiec Gallery showcases contemporary art and hosts exhibitions that contribute to Slovakia's vibrant cultural landscape.

Nature enthusiasts are drawn to Martin not only for its proximity to the Tatras but also for the picturesque landscapes of the surrounding region. The nearby Malá Fatra National Park boasts rugged mountains, dense forests, and pristine valleys, providing ample opportunities for hiking, skiing, and exploring the natural beauty of the area.

Culinary experiences in Martin offer a taste of Slovak cuisine, with local dishes such as bryndzové halušky (potato dumplings with sheep cheese) and kapustnica (sauerkraut soup) gracing the menus of local restaurants and eateries.

In conclusion, Martin, often regarded as the "Gateway to the Tatras," is a city that combines its role as a starting point for mountain adventures with its own rich cultural and historical heritage. Whether you're exploring its museums, admiring its architecture, or using it as a base for exploring the natural wonders of the Tatras and Malá Fatra, Martin offers a multifaceted experience that celebrates the beauty of Slovakia's northern region.

Poprad: Adventure Hub

Nestled in the foothills of the majestic Tatra Mountains, Poprad is a vibrant city that has earned its reputation as an adventure hub in Slovakia. With its stunning natural surroundings, a wide range of outdoor activities, and a rich cultural heritage, Poprad beckons travelers seeking thrilling experiences and a deep connection with nature.

The city's origins date back to medieval times when it served as a trade and administrative center. Over the centuries, Poprad evolved, blending its historical charm with modern amenities to become a gateway to the Tatras and an adventure enthusiast's paradise.

Poprad's proximity to the Tatra Mountains, part of the Carpathian range, is one of its defining features. The High Tatras, with their dramatic peaks, lush valleys, and pristine lakes, offer a playground for hikers, climbers, and nature lovers. Poprad serves as a convenient base for exploring this natural wonderland.

One of the city's iconic landmarks is the Church of St. Egidius, an elegant Gothic structure that graces the city center. Its soaring spire and intricate architecture make it a focal point of Poprad's skyline. The nearby Spisska Sobota district, with its well-preserved historic buildings, adds to the city's charm.

Poprad's cultural life is vibrant, with museums, galleries, and festivals that celebrate its heritage. The Tatranská Galéria, situated in a historic building, showcases contemporary and traditional art, reflecting the region's creative spirit. Throughout the year, the city hosts cultural events, from music festivals to craft fairs, providing entertainment for residents and visitors.

Outdoor enthusiasts flock to Poprad for its plethora of adventure opportunities. Hiking and trekking trails crisscross the Tatras, catering to all levels of experience. In winter, the region transforms into a winter wonderland, with ski resorts and snow-covered landscapes inviting skiers and snowboarders.

For adrenaline seekers, the Tatra Mountains offer rock climbing, mountaineering, and paragliding adventures. The Belianska Cave, with its striking limestone formations, provides a unique underground exploration experience. The AquaCity Poprad, a modern water park and wellness complex, offers relaxation and rejuvenation after a day of outdoor activities.

Poprad's culinary scene is a delightful journey into Slovak cuisine, with local dishes such as bryndzové halušky (potato dumplings with sheep cheese) and pirohy (dumplings) available in cozy restaurants and eateries.

In conclusion, Poprad, the adventure hub of Slovakia, invites travelers to immerse themselves in the wonders of the Tatra Mountains while experiencing the city's rich cultural heritage. Whether you're scaling mountain peaks, exploring historic streets, or indulging in local cuisine, Poprad offers an exhilarating and memorable experience that celebrates the beauty of Slovakia's northern region.

The History of Slovak Castles

Slovakia, a country nestled in the heart of Europe, is a land steeped in history and rich in cultural heritage. One of the most prominent aspects of Slovakia's historical landscape is its castles. These impressive fortifications dot the countryside and tell the tales of kings, knights, and centuries of change. As we delve into the history of Slovak castles, we'll uncover the stories of their rise, fall, and enduring legacy.

The history of Slovak castles can be traced back to ancient times when fortifications were built for protection against invading tribes and foreign powers. Over the centuries, as Slovakia became a crossroads of trade routes and a battleground for territorial disputes, these fortifications evolved into grand castles, fortresses, and citadels.

During the Middle Ages, the Kingdom of Hungary played a significant role in shaping the destiny of Slovakia, and many castles were constructed to defend its borders and exert control over the region. Some of the most notable castles from this era include Spiš Castle, the largest castle complex in Central Europe, and Červený Kameň Castle, known for its impressive architecture and historical significance.

The castles of Slovakia were not only military strongholds but also centers of culture and learning. They often housed noble families, and many were adorned with beautiful frescoes, intricate carvings, and elaborate gardens. Bojnice Castle, with its romantic architecture and lush surroundings, is a prime example of a castle that combined both defensive and aesthetic functions.

In the 16th century, Slovakia became part of the Habsburg Empire, and many castles were adapted to suit the needs of the ruling elite. Some castles, like Bratislava Castle overlooking the capital, underwent significant transformations to become grand residences rather than military fortifications.

The 17th and 18th centuries brought conflict and destruction to the region during various wars and uprisings. Many castles suffered damage and fell into disrepair during this tumultuous period. However, some were carefully preserved or restored, showcasing their historical significance.

In the 20th century, with the establishment of Czechoslovakia and the subsequent division of the country into Slovakia and the Czech Republic, many castles were opened to the public, allowing visitors to step back in time and explore their fascinating history.

Today, Slovakia's castles stand as a testament to the country's enduring legacy, offering a glimpse into the past and a sense of wonder for all who visit. Whether perched on rugged hills, nestled in lush valleys, or standing proudly in urban centers, these castles continue to captivate the imagination and remind us of Slovakia's rich and diverse history.

In conclusion, the history of Slovak castles is a journey through time, filled with tales of conquest, culture, and resilience. These magnificent fortifications, with their centuries-old walls and timeless stories, provide a window into the past and a connection to Slovakia's remarkable heritage. As we explore these castles, we embark on a historical adventure that reveals the enduring spirit of this enchanting country.

Slovak Fortifications and Defensive Structures

Slovakia, nestled in the heart of Europe, boasts a rich tapestry of historical fortifications and defensive structures that have played a crucial role in the region's history. From ancient hillforts to medieval castles and modern bunkers, these structures reflect the ever-changing dynamics of power, conflict, and the enduring need for protection.

The story of Slovak fortifications begins in prehistoric times when hillforts, strategically positioned on elevated terrain, provided early inhabitants with defensive advantages. These ancient settlements, constructed primarily from wood and earthworks, served as centers of trade and refuge from marauding tribes.

With the arrival of the Roman Empire in the 1st century AD, the region that is now Slovakia became a part of the Roman frontier, known as the Limes Romanus. Along this border, the Romans erected watchtowers and fortifications to guard against incursions from Germanic tribes. The remnants of these structures can still be seen in parts of modern-day Slovakia.

The Middle Ages marked a significant period of fortification construction, driven by the feudal system and the need for protection from invading forces. Castles, such as Spiš Castle and Devín Castle, became formidable strongholds, often perched atop rocky promontories or hills, offering commanding views of the surrounding landscape. These castles, constructed from stone and fortified with walls and towers, were symbols of power and control.

During the Ottoman-Habsburg wars in the 16th and 17th centuries, fortifications took on renewed importance as Slovakia found itself on the front lines of conflict. Impressive fortresses, like Komárno Fortress, were built to defend against the Ottoman Empire's advances. These fortifications featured moats, bastions, and thick walls to withstand artillery fire.

The 20th century brought a new chapter in the history of Slovak fortifications with the construction of bunkers and defensive lines during World War I and World War II. The Štúr Line, a system of border fortifications, was built to protect Czechoslovakia from potential aggression. These bunkers, often hidden in the rugged terrain, serve as a testament to the country's readiness for defense.

In the post-World War II era, Slovakia's fortifications underwent changes as the country's borders shifted and military strategies evolved. While many fortifications were abandoned or repurposed, some have been preserved as historical sites and museums, offering a glimpse into Slovakia's military past.

Today, Slovakia's fortifications and defensive structures stand as enduring reminders of the country's history, showcasing the ingenuity and determination of its people to safeguard their land and heritage. From ancient hillforts to modern bunkers, these structures provide a tangible link to Slovakia's past and serve as a testament to the resilience of its people in the face of challenges.

UNESCO World Heritage Sites

Slovakia, a country of remarkable natural beauty and rich cultural heritage, is home to several UNESCO World Heritage Sites that showcase its historical significance and outstanding landscapes. These sites have earned their place on the prestigious list due to their cultural, historical, and natural value, and they offer a window into the diverse and captivating aspects of Slovakia's heritage.

1.   Spiš Castle: This colossal medieval fortress, located in the eastern part of Slovakia, is one of the largest castle complexes in Europe. With its stunning architecture and strategic location overlooking the town of Spišské Podhradie, Spiš Castle is a testament to the power and influence of the Spiš region during the Middle Ages.

2.   Vlkolínec: Nestled in the Velká Fatra Mountains, Vlkolínec is a picturesque village that has preserved its traditional folk architecture and way of life. The well-preserved wooden houses, adorned with charming details, offer a glimpse into the rural heritage of Slovakia.

3.   Bardejov: The historic town of Bardejov, located in the northeastern part of the country, is a remarkable example of a medieval town with a well-preserved central square and fortifications. Its architecture, including the Gothic Church of St. Giles, reflects the rich history of the region.

4.   Caves of Aggtelek Karst and Slovak Karst: This transboundary UNESCO site, shared with Hungary, comprises a complex of limestone caves and underground passages. The Slovak part of this natural wonder is known for the Domica Cave, accessible to visitors and adorned with stunning stalactites and stalagmites.

5.   Levoča, Spišský Hrad, and the Associated Cultural Monuments: This UNESCO site encompasses the town of

Levoča, the Spiš Castle, and their surrounding cultural monuments. Levoča boasts the tallest wooden Gothic altar in the world, found in the Church of St. James, while Spiš Castle stands as a magnificent example of medieval fortification.

6.   Wooden Churches of the Slovak part of the Carpathian Mountain Area: This series of wooden churches, located in the Carpathian Mountains, represents the rich architectural and religious traditions of the region's communities. These churches, with their unique construction techniques and decorative elements, are a testament to the enduring cultural heritage of Slovakia.

7.   Dobsina Ice Cave: Tucked away in the Slovak Paradise National Park, the Dobsina Ice Cave is renowned for its ice formations and underground beauty. It's one of the most accessible ice caves in the world and provides a fascinating glimpse into the subterranean wonders of Slovakia.

8.   Primeval Beech Forests of the Carpathians and Other Regions of Europe: This UNESCO site encompasses a network of ancient beech forests across Europe, including parts of Slovakia. These pristine forests are not only biologically diverse but also hold cultural and ecological significance.

9.   Historic Town of Banská Štiavnica and the Technical Monuments in its Vicinity: Banská Štiavnica, a historic mining town in central Slovakia, showcases a unique blend of Renaissance architecture and mining heritage. Its mining landscapes and historical significance are celebrated through this UNESCO listing.

These UNESCO World Heritage Sites in Slovakia offer a glimpse into the country's rich history, cultural diversity, and breathtaking natural landscapes. They stand as a testament to Slovakia's commitment to preserving and showcasing its exceptional heritage for future generations to appreciate and cherish.

The Slovak Language

In the heart of Central Europe lies Slovakia, a country known not only for its stunning landscapes and rich cultural heritage but also for its unique language, Slovak. The Slovak language, a Slavic tongue, is an integral part of the nation's identity and history. Let's delve into the fascinating world of Slovak, its origins, characteristics, and significance in the tapestry of Slovakian culture.

Slovak belongs to the West Slavic branch of the Slavic language family, closely related to Czech, Polish, and Sorbian. It shares its linguistic roots with these languages but has developed its distinct characteristics over the centuries.

The story of the Slovak language can be traced back to the Slavic migrations and settlement of the region, which began around the 5th century AD. These early Slavs brought their languages with them, laying the foundation for what would become the Slovak language.

Throughout its history, Slovakia has been influenced by neighboring cultures and languages, including Hungarian, German, and Latin. These influences have left indelible marks on Slovak vocabulary and pronunciation, making it a language that reflects the country's diverse heritage.

One of the defining features of Slovak is its use of the Latin script, which was introduced by Christian missionaries in the 9th century. This script became the basis for the Slovak alphabet, which consists of 46 letters, including diacritics (accent marks) that modify the pronunciation of certain sounds.

Slovak grammar is characterized by a system of declensions, which determine the grammatical case of nouns, adjectives, and pronouns. There are seven grammatical cases in Slovak, each serving a specific purpose in sentence structure. The complexity of the grammatical cases can be challenging for learners but adds depth and precision to the language.

Slovak's vocabulary is rich and diverse, reflecting its historical and cultural influences. It has borrowed words from Latin, German, Hungarian, and other languages, adapting them to fit its phonetic and grammatical rules.

Slovak is the official language of Slovakia and is spoken by the majority of the population. It is also recognized as a minority language in some neighboring countries, such as the Czech Republic and Hungary, where Slovak-speaking communities exist.

In recent years, efforts have been made to promote and preserve the Slovak language. Language schools, cultural institutions, and media play a vital role in ensuring the language's vitality and relevance in a globalized world.

In conclusion, the Slovak language is a testament to the rich history and cultural diversity of Slovakia. It has evolved over centuries, absorbing influences from neighboring languages while retaining its unique character. Today, Slovak stands as a symbol of national identity and a key element in preserving the heritage and traditions of this captivating Central European nation.

Language Diversity in Slovakia

Slovakia, a country nestled in the heart of Europe, boasts a fascinating tapestry of languages and dialects that reflect its rich history and cultural complexity. While Slovak is the official language and widely spoken, the linguistic landscape of Slovakia is far from monolithic. Let's embark on a journey through the diverse linguistic mosaic that defines this Central European nation.

1. **Slovak**: At the forefront of Slovakia's linguistic identity is, of course, the Slovak language. As the official language, it is spoken by the majority of the population and is the medium of instruction in schools and government affairs. Slovak, a Slavic language, is known for its intricate grammatical structure, including the use of grammatical cases.

2. **Hungarian**: In the southern regions of Slovakia, particularly in areas along the Hungarian border, Hungarian is a significant minority language. The historical presence of Hungarian-speaking communities dates back centuries, and today, Hungarian remains an essential part of Slovakia's linguistic diversity.

3. **Rusyn**: In the northeastern part of Slovakia, particularly in the Prešov Region, Rusyn is spoken by the Rusyn minority. This East Slavic language has its roots in the Carpathian region and reflects the cultural heritage of the Rusyn community.

4. **Romani**: The Romani language, spoken by the Romani minority in Slovakia, adds another layer of linguistic diversity. The Romani people, who have a distinct cultural identity, maintain their language as an integral part of their heritage.

5. **Czech**: Due to historical ties between Slovakia and the Czech Republic, the Czech language is understood and spoken by many Slovaks. While it is not an official language, its familiarity is a result of the shared history of Czechoslovakia.

6. **German**: In some areas, especially in the western part of Slovakia near the Austrian border, the German language has had an influence. Historical connections with German-speaking communities have left traces of the language in local culture and place names.

7. **Polish and Ukrainian**: In border regions, particularly in the north, there are smaller communities of Poles and Ukrainians who maintain their languages and cultural traditions. These languages are often spoken within these communities and contribute to the linguistic diversity of the region.

8. **English and Other Foreign Languages**: In urban centers and among the younger generation, English is increasingly spoken and learned as a second language. Other foreign languages, such as French, Spanish, and Russian, are also taught in schools and used in various professional contexts.

The linguistic diversity in Slovakia is a testament to its historical ties with neighboring countries, as well as the presence of minority communities with their own linguistic traditions. While Slovak remains the dominant language and a symbol of national identity, the coexistence of these languages and dialects adds depth and richness to the cultural fabric of Slovakia.

In recent years, efforts have been made to promote multilingualism and preserve the linguistic heritage of minority communities. These initiatives aim to foster mutual respect and understanding among Slovakia's diverse linguistic groups, highlighting the country's commitment to inclusivity and cultural preservation.

Learning Slovak: Tips and Resources

Embarking on the journey to learn the Slovak language is an exciting endeavor that opens doors to the rich culture, history, and traditions of Slovakia. While Slovak, like any language, comes with its unique challenges, there are plenty of resources and strategies to help you along the way. In this chapter, we'll explore tips and resources to make your Slovak language learning experience fruitful and enjoyable.

1. **Start with the Basics**: Begin by learning the Slovak alphabet and pronunciation. Familiarize yourself with the unique diacritics (accent marks) that modify the sounds of certain letters. This foundation will be invaluable as you progress.
2. **Language Classes**: Consider enrolling in Slovak language classes, either in person or online. Many language schools and universities offer courses designed for beginners, intermediate learners, and advanced students.
3. **Language Apps and Websites**: Language learning apps like Duolingo, Babbel, and Memrise offer Slovak courses that you can access on your smartphone or computer. These apps are interactive and convenient for self-paced learning.
4. **Online Resources**: Explore websites and online forums dedicated to Slovak language learners. Websites like Transparent Language and Slovak Online offer lessons, exercises, and valuable insights into the language.
5. **Language Exchange Partners**: Connect with native Slovak speakers who are learning your native

language. Language exchange partners can help you practice speaking and understanding Slovak while you assist them with their language goals.

6. **Textbooks and Workbooks**: Invest in reputable Slovak language textbooks and workbooks. These materials provide structured lessons, grammar explanations, and exercises to reinforce your skills.

7. **Slovak Media**: Immerse yourself in the Slovak language by watching Slovak films, TV shows, and listening to Slovak radio and podcasts. Exposure to native speakers will improve your listening comprehension and accent.

8. **Language Tutors**: If you prefer one-on-one instruction, consider hiring a language tutor. Tutors can tailor lessons to your specific needs and provide personalized guidance.

9. **Practice Speaking**: Don't be shy about practicing your speaking skills. Engage in conversations with native speakers whenever possible. Join language clubs or conversation groups in your area.

10. **Language Certifications**: If you plan to use your Slovak language skills for professional or academic purposes, consider taking language proficiency exams like the Test of Slovak as a Foreign Language (TSUS).

11. **Travel to Slovakia**: If circumstances allow, visiting Slovakia can be a transformative language learning experience. Immersing yourself in the country's culture and language can accelerate your progress.

12. **Patience and Persistence**: Learning any language takes time and dedication. Be patient with yourself and stay committed to regular practice. Consistency is key to mastering Slovak.

13. **Cultural Understanding**: Learning the language is not just about words and grammar; it's also about

understanding the culture. Explore Slovak customs, traditions, and history to deepen your appreciation of the language.

14. **Online Communities**: Join online communities and forums where Slovak language learners share tips, experiences, and resources. You can seek advice, ask questions, and connect with fellow learners.

15. **Language Games and Quizzes**: Engage in language games, quizzes, and crossword puzzles to make learning more enjoyable and reinforce your vocabulary.

Remember that language learning is a personal journey, and what works best for one person may differ for another. Experiment with various resources and strategies to find the combination that suits your learning style and goals. Above all, stay motivated, and embrace the challenges as opportunities to grow and connect with the Slovak-speaking world. Learning Slovak is not just about acquiring a new skill; it's a gateway to a vibrant and unique culture waiting to be explored.

Slovak Folk Music and Dance

Slovakia, a country steeped in cultural richness and tradition, boasts a vibrant world of folk music and dance that reflects the soul of its people. These age-old traditions have been passed down through generations, and they continue to play a significant role in the cultural identity of Slovakia.

Folk Music: The Heartbeat of Tradition

Slovak folk music is a melodic tapestry that weaves together the stories, history, and emotions of the Slovak people. It's a living testament to the resilience of tradition in a rapidly changing world.

1. **Instruments**: Traditional Slovak folk music is brought to life by a range of instruments, including the fujara (a long wooden flute), the shepherd's flute (drbula), bagpipes, violins, and various percussion instruments. Each instrument has its unique sound and purpose, contributing to the rich tapestry of Slovak folk music.
2. **Styles**: Slovak folk music can be categorized into several regional styles, each with its distinct rhythms, melodies, and instruments. These regional variations highlight the diversity of Slovak culture.
3. **Lyrics and Themes**: The lyrics of Slovak folk songs often revolve around themes of love, nature, and everyday life. These songs tell stories of the past and serve as a connection to the country's rural roots.

4. **Dances**: Slovak folk music is inseparable from traditional dances. These dances, such as the kolo (circle dance), horehronský čardáš, and verbuňk, are performed at various celebrations, festivals, and cultural events. The intricate footwork and lively music create an enchanting spectacle.

Folk Dance: A Celebration of Life

Slovak folk dance is a dynamic and spirited expression of Slovak culture. It's not merely a performance but a communal celebration that brings people together in joy and unity.

1. **Costumes**: Slovak folk dancers wear colorful and ornate costumes that are specific to their regions. These costumes are not only a visual delight but also an essential part of preserving the authenticity of the dances.
2. **Celebrations and Festivals**: Folk dances are an integral part of Slovak celebrations and festivals. Whether it's a wedding, a harvest festival, or a holiday, you'll find folk dancers taking center stage, captivating audiences with their exuberance.
3. **Influence on Contemporary Arts**: The influence of Slovak folk dance extends beyond tradition. It has inspired contemporary dance forms and even found its way into modern artistic expressions, bridging the gap between the old and the new.
4. **Preserving Tradition**: Folk music and dance are cherished in Slovakia, and efforts are made to ensure their preservation. Folk ensembles and cultural organizations work diligently to teach these traditions to the younger generation.

5. **UNESCO Recognition**: Some Slovak folk traditions have earned recognition as UNESCO Intangible Cultural Heritage. This acknowledgment highlights their significance in preserving the country's cultural heritage.

Slovak folk music and dance are not relics of the past but living traditions that continue to evolve and thrive. They embody the spirit and resilience of the Slovak people, serving as a bridge between the past and the future. Whether you're watching a lively dance performance or listening to the soulful melodies of folk music, you're immersing yourself in the heart and soul of Slovakia's vibrant cultural heritage.

Traditional Slovak Clothing

Traditional Slovak clothing is a vivid tapestry of history, culture, and regional identity. Rooted in centuries-old traditions, these garments are a testament to the rich heritage of the Slovak people, reflecting the diversity and uniqueness of various regions across the country.

Men's Attire

In rural Slovakia, the clothing worn by men is not just a matter of style but also a reflection of their daily lives and occupations.

1. **Shirt (Košeľa)**: The basic garment for men is the košeľa, a white linen shirt with intricate embroidery. The patterns on the shirt often signify the region or village of the wearer.
2. **Vest (Vestka)**: Over the shirt, men often wear a vest called a vestka, which is also adorned with colorful embroidery. The vest is typically made of wool and provides warmth during the colder months.
3. **Trousers (Nohavice)**: Traditional trousers are usually made of wool or linen, designed to be durable and comfortable for daily work.
4. **Sash (Paštika)**: To complete the ensemble, men wear a paštika, a wide sash that is tied around the waist. The sash is not only decorative but also functional, helping to secure the trousers.
5. **Footwear**: In rural areas, leather boots are commonly worn. These boots are sturdy and suitable for various outdoor activities.

Women's Attire

Traditional Slovak women's clothing is a symphony of color and intricate detail, often reflecting the wearer's marital status and region.

1. **Blouse (Kroj)**: The central piece of women's traditional clothing is the kroj, a blouse that features exquisite embroidery. The style and colors of the blouse can vary significantly between regions.
2. **Skirt (Sukňa)**: The sukňa, or skirt, is worn with the kroj and is typically made of wool or linen. The length and design of the skirt can vary depending on the region.
3. **Apron (Fartúch)**: An apron called a fartúch is worn over the skirt. Like other elements of the traditional outfit, the apron is adorned with embroidery.
4. **Headwear**: Women often wear head coverings, such as scarves or bonnets, which can also vary by region. The designs can be quite intricate and are often symbolic.
5. **Footwear**: Traditional women's footwear includes leather shoes or boots, which are practical for both work and celebrations.

Occasions and Symbolism

Traditional Slovak clothing is not only beautiful but also deeply symbolic. The choice of colors, patterns, and even the presence of certain accessories can convey a wealth of information about the wearer. These garments are often worn during special occasions and festivals, preserving the cultural identity and connecting people to their roots.

It's important to note that while traditional clothing is still cherished and worn during festivals and celebrations, it has become less common in everyday life. However, the pride in this cultural heritage remains strong, and the art of crafting and preserving traditional Slovak clothing is passed down through generations.

In conclusion, traditional Slovak clothing is a living art form that encapsulates the essence of Slovak culture and history. The intricate embroidery, vibrant colors, and regional variations all come together to tell the story of a resilient and diverse nation. While the styles may have evolved over time, the significance of these garments in preserving Slovak identity remains unwavering.

Slovak Folklore and Superstitions

The rich tapestry of Slovak culture is intricately woven with folklore and superstitions that have been passed down through generations. These beliefs and traditions provide a fascinating glimpse into the collective psyche of the Slovak people, connecting them to their ancestors and the natural world around them.

Folklore: Tales of Old

1. **Legends and Myths**: Slovak folklore is replete with captivating legends and myths that explain the origins of natural phenomena, landmarks, and even the country itself. These stories often feature mythical creatures, heroes, and moral lessons.
2. **Fairy Tales**: Slovak fairy tales, much like those found in other cultures, are filled with magical elements, enchanting creatures, and brave protagonists. They are told to entertain, educate, and inspire imagination.
3. **Oral Tradition**: For centuries, folklore was primarily an oral tradition, passed down from one generation to the next through storytelling. It was a way to preserve the history and wisdom of the people.
4. **Regional Variations**: Slovakia's diverse regions have their own unique folklore, with distinct stories, characters, and traditions. This regional diversity adds depth and richness to the overall tapestry of Slovak folklore.

Superstitions: The Power of Belief

1. **Warding off Evil**: Superstitions in Slovakia often revolve around protecting oneself from evil spirits and bad luck. Common practices include carrying lucky charms, such as horseshoes or garlic, to ward off negative forces.

2. **Celestial Signs**: The position of the stars and celestial events has long been believed to influence human fate. For example, eclipses were seen as omens, and certain lunar phases were thought to impact a person's health.

3. **Cultural Celebrations**: Many superstitions are tied to specific cultural celebrations and events, such as weddings and holidays. These rituals are believed to ensure good fortune and happiness.

4. **Nature's Signs**: Folk wisdom often involves interpreting natural signs, such as the behavior of animals or the appearance of certain plants. These signs were used to predict the weather, harvests, and even the outcome of important endeavors.

5. **Life Milestones**: Superstitions are also prevalent during significant life events, such as births, marriages, and funerals. These rituals are meant to protect individuals and ensure a smooth transition through life's milestones.

6. **Preserving Traditions**: While some superstitions may seem quaint or outdated in the modern world, they continue to be upheld as a way of preserving cultural heritage and connecting with the past.

Slovak folklore and superstitions are not relics of the past but living traditions that continue to be celebrated and observed in various forms. They offer insight into the values, beliefs, and aspirations of the Slovak people, providing a bridge between the past and the present. Whether it's listening to enchanting folktales or participating in age-old rituals, experiencing Slovak folklore is a captivating journey into the heart and soul of this vibrant culture.

Cultural Diversity in Slovakia

Slovakia, nestled in the heart of Europe, is a country renowned for its rich cultural tapestry. It's a land where diverse traditions, languages, and histories have merged over centuries, creating a unique mosaic of identities that reflects the country's complex and fascinating cultural diversity.

Historical Influences

To understand the cultural diversity of Slovakia, we must delve into its historical roots, which have shaped the multifaceted nature of the nation.

1. **Habsburg Empire**: Slovakia spent centuries under the rule of the Habsburg Empire, which had a profound impact on its culture. The Austro-Hungarian monarchy left behind a legacy of architecture, language, and culinary traditions that still resonate today.
2. **Hungarian Influence**: The close proximity to Hungary led to a significant Hungarian influence on the southern regions of Slovakia. Hungarian traditions, language, and cuisine are integral to the culture of this area.
3. **German Settlements**: Historical German settlements in parts of Slovakia have contributed to a German cultural presence, with distinct traditions and dialects still visible in some communities.

Language Diversity

Language plays a pivotal role in Slovakia's cultural diversity, with multiple languages spoken across the country.

1. **Slovak**: Slovak is the official language and is spoken by the majority of the population. It's a Slavic language with a rich literary tradition.
2. **Hungarian**: Hungarian is a significant minority language, predominantly spoken in southern Slovakia, particularly in regions near the Hungarian border.
3. **Rusyn**: In the eastern part of Slovakia, the Rusyn language is spoken by the Rusyn minority, preserving their unique cultural heritage.

Religious Diversity

Religion has also played a vital role in shaping Slovakia's cultural landscape.

1. **Catholicism**: The majority of Slovaks are Catholic, and the influence of the Catholic Church is deeply embedded in the culture, from religious festivals to architecture.
2. **Protestantism**: Protestant communities, particularly in the north and east, have their own religious traditions and customs.
3. **Orthodoxy**: Eastern Orthodox Christianity is practiced by the Rusyn minority, with distinct religious ceremonies and iconography.

Cultural Celebrations

Slovakia's cultural diversity is celebrated through a multitude of festivals and events that showcase various traditions.

1. **Folk Festivals**: Throughout the year, Slovakia hosts numerous folk festivals that feature traditional music, dance, and costumes from different regions.
2. **Religious Celebrations**: Catholic and Protestant holidays are observed with religious processions, feasts, and ceremonies, while Eastern Orthodox traditions have their unique religious celebrations.
3. **Cultural Heritage**: Museums, galleries, and cultural institutions across Slovakia work tirelessly to preserve and promote the diverse cultural heritage of the country.

Contemporary Challenges and Opportunities

In the modern era, Slovakia faces the challenge of maintaining its cultural diversity while embracing globalization and technological advancements. However, it also presents an opportunity for the nation to share its rich cultural heritage with the world.

Slovakia's cultural diversity is a source of pride and a testament to the resilience and adaptability of its people. It's a nation where different cultures coexist, creating a harmonious blend that is as captivating as it is unique. Exploring Slovakia's cultural diversity is like embarking on a journey through time, where centuries of history and tradition come together to paint a vibrant and ever-evolving picture of a nation at the crossroads of Europe.

Slovak Sports and Athletes

Slovakia, a country nestled in the heart of Europe, boasts a rich sports culture that has produced remarkable athletes across various disciplines. From the thrill of winter sports in the Tatra Mountains to the passion for soccer on the green fields, Slovak sports have left an indelible mark on the global sporting stage.

Winter Sports Dominance

1. **Ice Hockey**: Ice hockey is undoubtedly one of Slovakia's most beloved sports. The nation's passion for the game is evident in its enthusiastic fan base and the success of the Slovak national team in international competitions. Slovak ice hockey players have made a significant impact in the NHL, with legends like Peter Šťastný and more recent stars like Zdeno Chára and Marián Hossa.

2. **Biathlon and Cross-Country Skiing**: Slovakia's stunning mountainous terrain provides the perfect backdrop for winter sports like biathlon and cross-country skiing. Athletes like Anastasia Kuzmina, who won multiple Olympic gold medals in biathlon, have become national heroes.

3. **Alpine Skiing**: The High Tatras offer challenging slopes for alpine skiing. Slovak skiers like Petra Vlhová have earned international recognition with their remarkable performances on the World Cup circuit.

Summer Sports Success

1. **Cycling**: Slovak cyclists like Peter Sagan have achieved global acclaim. Sagan, known for his incredible sprinting abilities, has won multiple Tour de France stages and earned the title of World Road Race Champion.
2. **Tennis**: Dominika Cibulková and Daniela Hantuchová have represented Slovakia on the international tennis scene. Cibulková reached the finals of the Australian Open, showcasing the country's prowess in individual sports.
3. **Canoeing and Kayaking**: Slovakia has a strong tradition of success in canoeing and kayaking, particularly in slalom events. Michal Martikán, a legend in the sport, has won multiple Olympic gold medals and World Championship titles.

Football and Other Team Sports

1. **Football (Soccer)**: While ice hockey often takes center stage, soccer is also popular in Slovakia. The national team has participated in international competitions like the FIFA World Cup and UEFA European Championships. Notable players like Marek Hamšík have played in top European leagues.
2. **Basketball**: Slovak basketball players have made their mark in European competitions and the NBA. Radoslav Nesterovič and Dominik Raab are among those who have represented Slovakia on the hardwood.
3. **Handball**: Handball enjoys popularity, with both men's and women's national teams competing on the international stage.

Olympic Achievements

Slovakia has a proud Olympic tradition, with athletes competing in a wide range of disciplines. The country's athletes have earned numerous medals, particularly in shooting, canoeing, and water polo.

Sports Culture and Legacy

Sports are deeply ingrained in Slovak culture, with local communities supporting their athletes with pride. Sporting events, from local competitions to international championships, are celebrated with enthusiasm and camaraderie.

In conclusion, Slovakia's sports and athletes have made their mark on the global stage, achieving success and recognition in a wide array of disciplines. From the icy rinks of ice hockey to the challenging slopes of alpine skiing, from the pedal-pounding action of cycling to the precision of biathlon, Slovak athletes continue to inspire and unite the nation through their dedication and remarkable achievements in the world of sports.

Transportation and Infrastructure

Slovakia, situated in the heart of Europe, boasts a well-developed transportation and infrastructure network that plays a pivotal role in connecting the nation with its neighbors and the wider world. This chapter explores the various facets of Slovakia's transportation systems and the essential infrastructure that supports its economic and social development.

Road Networks

Slovakia boasts an extensive road network that facilitates both domestic and international travel. The road infrastructure includes highways, expressways, and well-maintained national roads. The D1 highway, running from Bratislava in the west to Košice in the east, serves as the country's primary east-west corridor. The highway network also connects Slovakia to neighboring countries like Austria, Hungary, Poland, and the Czech Republic, fostering cross-border trade and tourism.

Railways

Slovakia's railway system is an integral part of its transportation landscape. The country's railways are well-connected to European rail networks, making train travel a convenient and efficient mode of transportation. Major railway lines link cities like Bratislava, Žilina, Košice, and Banská Bystrica. The electrified railway lines offer sustainable and reliable transportation options for both passengers and freight.

Air Travel

Slovakia is served by several international airports, with the Bratislava Airport (M. R. Štefánik Airport) being the busiest. This airport provides connectivity to major European cities and serves as a gateway for travelers arriving in Slovakia. Other regional airports, such as Košice International Airport, offer domestic and international flights, contributing to the country's accessibility.

Public Transportation

Slovakia has a well-developed public transportation system that includes buses and trams in cities and towns. Bratislava, the capital city, has an efficient public transport network that eases the daily commute for residents. Moreover, Slovakia's public transportation connects even remote villages, ensuring accessibility for all citizens.

River Transport

The Danube River, which flows through Slovakia, serves as an important waterway for transporting goods. Ports along the river facilitate trade and cargo transportation, making it a crucial part of the country's logistics infrastructure.

Infrastructure Investment

Slovakia has consistently invested in its infrastructure to improve connectivity and support economic growth. EU funding has played a significant role in modernizing transportation networks and upgrading existing infrastructure. These investments have led to improved road safety, reduced travel times, and enhanced mobility for both people and goods.

Challenges and Sustainability

While Slovakia's transportation and infrastructure systems have seen significant improvements, challenges remain. Managing traffic congestion in urban areas, maintaining aging infrastructure, and ensuring sustainable and environmentally friendly transportation solutions are ongoing priorities for the country.

In conclusion, Slovakia's transportation and infrastructure networks serve as the arteries of the nation, connecting its diverse regions and enabling economic growth and cultural exchange. As the country continues to invest in modernization and sustainability, it is poised to further enhance its position as a vital hub in the heart of Europe, where road, rail, air, and river networks converge to facilitate the movement of people and goods, supporting the nation's progress and development.

Slovak Education System

The education system in Slovakia is a cornerstone of the nation's development, fostering a well-educated populace and contributing to the country's growth and innovation. In this chapter, we delve into the structure, characteristics, and key aspects of the Slovak education system.

Structure of Education

The Slovak education system is divided into several stages, each with its own unique features and objectives.

1. **Early Childhood Education**: Early childhood education in Slovakia is not compulsory but widely available. It typically includes kindergartens and preschools that focus on the social and cognitive development of young children.
2. **Primary Education**: Primary education is mandatory for children between the ages of 6 and 16. It consists of nine grades and provides a broad foundation in subjects such as mathematics, languages (Slovak and typically one foreign language), science, and physical education.
3. **Secondary Education**: After completing primary education, students can pursue various paths in secondary education. The most common are:
   - **Gymnasium**: Gymnasiums offer a general education with a strong emphasis on academic subjects, preparing students for university entrance exams.
   - **Secondary Vocational Schools**: These schools provide specialized education in

various fields, including technical, economic, and vocational subjects, enabling students to acquire practical skills for specific careers.

4. **Tertiary Education**: Tertiary education in Slovakia includes universities and colleges. Universities offer bachelor's, master's, and doctoral programs across a wide range of disciplines. Comenius University in Bratislava is one of the oldest and most prestigious institutions in the country.

Language of Instruction

Slovak is the primary language of instruction in schools across all levels. However, foreign language instruction is also a crucial part of the curriculum, with English, German, and French being some of the most commonly taught languages.

Education Reforms

Slovakia has implemented various reforms to improve its education system. These reforms have aimed to enhance the quality of education, introduce modern teaching methods, and align the system with European standards. Efforts have also been made to address issues such as educational inequality and early school leaving.

Challenges and Opportunities

Despite progress in the education sector, challenges persist. These include disparities in educational outcomes among different regions, the need for updated infrastructure, and adapting to the demands of a rapidly changing job market. However, Slovakia's commitment to education and its investments in research and development present opportunities for growth and innovation.

Higher Education and Research

Slovakia's higher education institutions contribute significantly to research and development. These institutions engage in scientific research and collaborate with international partners, making valuable contributions to various fields.

In conclusion, the Slovak education system plays a vital role in shaping the nation's future by equipping its citizens with the knowledge and skills needed to succeed in a dynamic world. As Slovakia continues to invest in education and embrace educational reforms, it is positioning itself as a knowledge-based society that values learning, innovation, and the pursuit of excellence.

Healthcare in Slovakia

Healthcare is a fundamental aspect of any society, and in Slovakia, it holds great importance in ensuring the well-being of its citizens. In this chapter, we explore the healthcare system in Slovakia, its characteristics, and the key elements that make it an integral part of the nation's social fabric.

Universal Healthcare

Slovakia operates a universal healthcare system, which means that access to healthcare services is guaranteed to all citizens and residents. This system is funded primarily through compulsory health insurance contributions from both employees and employers. It ensures that every Slovakian has access to essential medical care regardless of their financial status.

Healthcare Providers

The healthcare landscape in Slovakia comprises a network of public and private healthcare providers. Public healthcare facilities are generally funded by the state and are accessible to all insured individuals. These include hospitals, clinics, and primary care centers. Private healthcare providers also play a significant role in delivering medical services, often catering to those who opt for private insurance or are willing to pay for services out of pocket.

Primary and Specialized Care

Primary care in Slovakia is provided by general practitioners and pediatricians. Patients usually consult with these primary care physicians first, who then refer them to specialists if needed. Specialized care is delivered by medical specialists who focus on various fields, including cardiology, orthopedics, gynecology, and more.

Health Insurance

As mentioned earlier, health insurance is mandatory for all employed individuals in Slovakia. It covers a wide range of medical services, including hospital stays, doctor's visits, medications, and preventive care. Additionally, there is the option to purchase supplementary private health insurance to access additional services or reduce waiting times for certain procedures.

Pharmaceuticals and Medications

Slovakia has a well-regulated pharmaceutical industry that ensures the availability of essential medications. Prescription medications are available through pharmacies, and patients often need a prescription from a healthcare provider to obtain certain drugs. The healthcare system covers a portion of medication costs, with patients contributing a co-payment.

Healthcare Challenges

While Slovakia's healthcare system provides comprehensive coverage, it faces challenges that require attention and reform. Some of these challenges include:

- Uneven distribution of healthcare resources, with urban areas having better access to healthcare facilities than rural regions.
- Waiting times for certain medical procedures and specialist consultations can be long.
- A need for further investments in healthcare infrastructure and modernization.
- Addressing disparities in healthcare outcomes among different population groups.

Despite these challenges, Slovakia's healthcare system continues to evolve and adapt to meet the changing needs of its population. Government initiatives and ongoing reforms aim to improve the quality and accessibility of healthcare services.

Health and Well-Being

The health and well-being of the Slovak population are of paramount importance. The country encourages healthy lifestyles through education and public health campaigns, promoting physical activity, balanced nutrition, and regular health check-ups.

In conclusion, healthcare in Slovakia is a fundamental right for all citizens and residents, ensuring that they have access to medical services when needed. The system, while facing its share of challenges, is an essential pillar of the country's commitment to the health and welfare of its people. As Slovakia continues to invest in healthcare infrastructure and improvements, it strives to provide high-quality medical care to its population for generations to come.

Tourism in Slovakia

Slovakia, nestled in the heart of Europe, is a hidden gem waiting to be explored by travelers seeking natural beauty, rich history, and a unique cultural experience. In this chapter, we embark on a journey through the diverse and captivating world of tourism in Slovakia.

Natural Wonders

Slovakia's landscape is a tapestry of natural wonders that will leave any nature enthusiast in awe. The Carpathian Mountains dominate the northern and central parts of the country, with the High Tatras standing proudly as the tallest peaks. These mountains offer a haven for hikers, skiers, and mountaineers, with pristine lakes, rugged trails, and stunning vistas at every turn.

Slovakia is blessed with numerous national parks, each offering its own unique charm. The Slovak Paradise National Park boasts intricate gorges and lush forests, perfect for adventurous hikers. The Slovenský Raj (Slovak Paradise) is a natural wonderland with trails leading through canyons, waterfalls, and unique rock formations.

Historic and Picturesque Cities

Slovakia's cities are a blend of history, culture, and modernity. The capital, Bratislava, sits on the banks of the Danube River and exudes old-world charm. Its medieval Old Town, crowned by Bratislava Castle, is a testament to the city's rich history. Stroll through narrow cobblestone streets, visit charming cafes, and soak in the atmosphere of this vibrant city.

Košice, Slovakia's second-largest city, is a treasure trove of Gothic and Baroque architecture. Its well-preserved historic center is a joy to explore, with landmarks like St. Elisabeth Cathedral and the beautifully adorned State Theatre.

Banská Štiavnica, a UNESCO World Heritage Site, is a town steeped in mining history. Its unique urban layout and historic mining structures offer a glimpse into Slovakia's past.

Cultural Heritage

Slovakia's cultural heritage is as diverse as its landscapes. The country's folklore is alive and well, celebrated through music, dance, and traditional festivals. Folk architecture can be seen in charming wooden churches, colorful cottages, and open-air museums.

Slovak cuisine is a delightful journey of flavors, influenced by its Central European neighbors. Try traditional dishes like bryndzové halušky (dumplings with sheep cheese) or kapustnica (cabbage soup) for a taste of authentic Slovak flavors.

Outdoor Adventures

Slovakia is an outdoor adventurer's paradise. The Tatras offer skiing and snowboarding in the winter and hiking and biking in the summer. Rafting, kayaking, and caving are popular activities in the country's many rivers and caves.

The country's extensive network of cycling trails and well-marked hiking routes make it accessible to both beginners and seasoned adventurers.

Historical Landmarks

Slovakia is dotted with historical landmarks, from ancient castles perched on hilltops to fortified churches and medieval towns. Spiš Castle, another UNESCO World Heritage Site, is one of the largest castle complexes in Europe, while Orava Castle is perched majestically overlooking a reservoir.

Conclusion

Slovakia, with its natural beauty, rich history, and vibrant culture, offers a unique and unforgettable travel experience. Whether you're an outdoor enthusiast, history buff, or simply seeking a peaceful escape, Slovakia has something to offer every traveler. Its warm hospitality and the sense of discovery that comes with exploring its hidden treasures make it a destination worth exploring. So pack your bags and get ready to uncover the many wonders of Slovakia.

Must-Visit Tourist Attractions

Slovakia is a country brimming with captivating attractions that cater to a wide range of interests and preferences. In this chapter, we'll take a journey through some of the must-visit tourist attractions that will leave you with lasting memories of this beautiful and culturally rich nation.

Bratislava Castle

The iconic Bratislava Castle, perched on a hill overlooking the capital city, is an essential stop on your Slovak adventure. Dating back to the 9th century, this historic fortress has witnessed centuries of history and is now home to the Slovak National Museum. The panoramic views from the castle grounds are breathtaking, offering a stunning vista of the city and the Danube River.

Spiš Castle

Spiš Castle, a UNESCO World Heritage Site, is one of the largest castle complexes in Europe. Located in the Spiš region, this medieval marvel boasts a dramatic hilltop location and offers visitors a glimpse into Slovakia's storied past. Explore its extensive grounds, visit the castle museum, and take in the awe-inspiring views of the surrounding landscape.

High Tatras

The High Tatras, the tallest mountains in Slovakia, are a haven for nature enthusiasts and outdoor adventurers. Whether you're an avid hiker, skier, or simply seeking a serene escape, the High Tatras have it all. Explore the picturesque valleys, pristine lakes, and rugged peaks. In the winter, the region transforms into a snow-covered wonderland, perfect for skiing and snowboarding.

Slovak Paradise National Park

Slovak Paradise National Park, or Slovenský Raj, is a natural paradise for hikers and nature lovers. Its unique landscapes feature deep gorges, limestone plateaus, and stunning waterfalls. The park is crisscrossed with hiking trails and wooden ladders, allowing you to venture deep into its enchanting terrain.

Devin Castle

Just a short trip from Bratislava, Devin Castle is a historical gem that sits at the confluence of the Danube and Morava rivers. Its strategic location has made it a site of significance throughout history. Explore its ruins, take in the river views, and learn about its rich history at the on-site museum.

Orava Castle

Orava Castle, dramatically perched atop a hill, is another Slovakian castle that will transport you back in time. Its picturesque location overlooking the Orava River and the surrounding countryside makes it a favorite among photographers. Inside, you'll find a museum that delves into the history and culture of the region.

Spa Towns

Slovakia is known for its soothing spa towns, where you can relax and rejuvenate. Piestany is renowned for its thermal springs and therapeutic mud, while Bardejov offers a beautifully preserved medieval old town and therapeutic mineral waters.

Vlkolínec

Vlkolínec is a UNESCO World Heritage Site and a perfectly preserved folk village. Walking through its charming lanes, you'll feel like you've stepped back in time. The traditional wooden houses and their well-maintained gardens provide a glimpse into rural Slovak life of the past.

Conclusion

Slovakia's tourist attractions are as diverse as the country itself, offering a blend of history, natural beauty, and cultural richness. Whether you're exploring ancient castles, hiking in the majestic mountains, or soaking in the healing waters of a spa town, Slovakia's attractions are sure to leave a lasting impression on any traveler. So, as you plan your Slovak adventure, be sure to include these must-visit destinations in your itinerary for an unforgettable experience.

Epilogue

As we come to the end of our journey through the pages of "Everything You Need to Know about Slovakia," it's time to reflect on the rich tapestry of this remarkable country. Slovakia, nestled in the heart of Europe, may be small in size, but it is abundant in history, culture, and natural beauty.

Throughout the chapters of this book, we've explored the geographical diversity of Slovakia, from its towering mountains in the High Tatras to the serene beauty of its national parks. We've traced its historical roots, from its medieval past as part of the Kingdom of Hungary to the turbulent years of World War I and II, and the Velvet Revolution that led to its independence.

We've delved into the political structure and economic development of the country, learning about its government, industries, and educational and healthcare systems. We've savored the flavors of Slovak cuisine and learned about the importance of traditions and folklore in the lives of its people.

From Bratislava, the vibrant capital city, to the historic gems of Kosice, Presov, Banska Bystrica, Nitra, Trnava, Martin, Poprad, and countless others, we've traversed the cities and towns that make up the mosaic of Slovakia.

We've marveled at the architectural wonders and landmarks that dot the landscape, from ancient castles and fortifications to UNESCO World Heritage Sites that bear witness to the nation's heritage.

The chapters on language, diversity, and learning have illuminated the linguistic and cultural richness of Slovakia, offering insights into the mosaic of languages and the resources available for those eager to embrace the Slovak way of life.

We've celebrated the vibrant traditions, festivals, music, dance, literature, and art that define Slovak culture and creativity. We've explored the role of religion and spirituality in shaping the nation's identity.

Slovakia's commitment to environmental conservation has been highlighted, as well as its natural wonders, wildlife, and the efforts made to protect and preserve its precious ecosystems.

We've embraced the warmth of Slovak hospitality and discovered the joy of celebrations and festivals that bring people together to revel in their shared traditions.

Sports and athleticism have been a source of national pride, with Slovak athletes making their mark on the global stage in various disciplines.

Transportation and infrastructure have played a pivotal role in shaping the country's connectivity, making it accessible to travelers from around the world.

The chapters on education and healthcare have shed light on the systems in place to nurture the well-being and development of Slovak citizens.

And finally, we've embarked on a virtual tour of Slovakia's top tourist attractions, urging travelers to explore its hidden gems and iconic sites.

As we conclude this journey, it's clear that Slovakia is a nation with a rich past, a vibrant present, and a promising future. Its unique blend of natural beauty, cultural heritage, and warm hospitality make it a destination worth exploring.